Praise for Flourishing Kin

"Immense gratitude to the energy of the nahual kat for giving our dear sister Yuria Celidwen the authority to share the wisdom of our Peoples. In the twelve chapters of *Flourishing Kin*, the voice of the great Spirit gives life to the distinct and diverse cosmovisions of our Indigenous Peoples of the world. I raise my word to the eternal infinite of the Divine Creator, the heart of the Skies, the heart of Mother Earth to bless the words in this book. May they connect with the reader to awaken our practices, revitalize our cultures, and attain harmony with Mother Earth. This book is an opening path! Matiox Ajaw jun, kamul, Ajaw, one, two, and three times thank you."

Angelina Sacbajá Tun
sacred knowledge keeper of the Maya Kaqchikel, International
Council of Thirteen Indigenous Grandmothers, and
leader of traditional Indigenous midwifery

"Spoken as a true sage, Yuria Celidwen has voiced a mindful story of prayer, hope, and remembrance of the Indigenous Spirit of Mindfulness. It is a story of a Spirit that still exists and whispers to us its message of love, kindness, and reverence for undying Spirit of Life. A pleasure to read and an inspiration for all to move forward to mindfully face the intractable challenges of our times!"

Gregory Cajete, PhD
former director of Native American Studies at the University
of New Mexico and author of *Native Science*

"Indigenous cultures have managed to live sustainably in their natural habitats for many thousands of years. They know things about life and land, kin and relationality, nature and sustainability that we humans need to wake up to and instantiate on every level, from the personal to the planetary. In *Flourishing Kin*, Yuria Celidwen shows herself to be a weaver of worlds, articulating the original Indigenous sacredness and interconnectedness of all life on this precious planet of ours, and the need for us as humans at this moment to live our way into the very real strands of relationality and kinship that might sustainably right long-standing wrongs and injustices and repair the harm, the exploitation, and the grief that our othering and impulses to capitalize, extract, and dominate inevitably lead to. The only way to do this, of course, is for humanity to wake up to its deepest embodied and enacted nature, and this is what this book might just catalyze and nurture in us going forward."

Jon Kabat-Zinn, PhD
founder of Mindfulness-Based Stress Reduction and author
of *Full Catastrophe Living* and *Coming to Our Senses*

"The essential truth reflected in this heartfelt and scholarly work is the powerful Indigenous wisdom of community. Yuria shows how much the beauty and vision of the collective has been neglected in the individual focus on contemplative practice and how important it is to awaken together with all!"

Jack Kornfield
cofounder of the Spirit Rock Center and the Insight
Meditation Society and author of *A Path with Heart*

"Our ecological crisis and global violence arise from us humans forgetting our belonging, our embeddedness in the web of life. Drawing on the vast repository of wisdom from Indigenous contemplative traditions, Yuria Celidwen offers us a pathway of awakening from an individual identity to the cellular realization of our collective belonging. This powerful guide is a spiritual transmission that flows from Yuria's own Indigenous roots and directly evokes a reverence for the sacredness and connectedness of all life. *Flourishing Kin* is profoundly relevant to our times, an urgently needed medicine for planetary flourishing."

Tara Brach
founder of the Insight Meditation Community of
Washington, DC, and author of *Radical Compassion*

"Dr. Celidwen has made a profound contribution to the study of human flourishing, which has traditionally ignored rich Indigenous traditions and focused on the individual. *Flourishing Kin* provides a deeply needed antidote by bridging Western and Indigenous science and centering on relationality, interdependence, mutuality, and the meaning inherent in all living phenomena. Celidwen makes a convincing case that only by striving for the flourishing of all our kin can we achieve true well-being."

john a. powell
director of the Othering & Belonging Institute
and author of *The Power of Bridging*

"In this brilliant and stirring book, Indigenous scientist, activist, and teacher Dr. Yuria Celidwen will take you on a powerful and inspiring tour of Indigenous histories, cultures, and wisdom, all brought together in a moving synthesis of scholarship, personal story, and practice. Reading this book will transform how you live your life, orienting you to your deep relatedness to nature and all living forms and pointing you to a path toward collective flourishing, so urgently needed during these times of crisis."

Dacher Keltner, PhD
Distinguished Professor of psychology at UC Berkeley, founding
director of the Greater Good Science Center, and author of *Awe*

"This extraordinary book brings us to the very heart of what it means to flourish in our world today and to nourish flourishing in our world. Drawn from the deep roots of Indigenous wisdom, it is a brilliant light in our imperiled world."

Roshi Joan Halifax, PhD
abbot, Upaya Zen Center, and author of *Being with Dying*

"Yuria Celidwen is an Indigenous healer, scholar, and scientist of Nahua and Maya heritage from Chiapas, Mexico. *Flourishing Kin* is her extraordinary book that blends the ancient wisdom of her Elders and Mother Earth with modern science and presents a sorely needed recipe for reverence, respect, reparations, and more to help restore our balance with our planet and with each other. She provides simple, accessible Indigenous contemplative practices that are relevant for us all and will help us to reconnect with our Spirit, our kin, and our planet. A very timely manifesto that will be of great benefit to our future."

Richard J. Davidson, PhD
founder and director of the Center for Healthy Minds and coauthor
of *New York Times* bestseller *The Emotional Life of Your Brain*

Flourishing Kin

Flourishing Kin

Indigenous Wisdom for Collective Well-Being

Yuria Celidwen, PhD

sounds true

BOULDER, COLORADO

Sounds True
Boulder, CO

This book is not intended as a substitute for the medical recommendations of physicians
or other health-care providers. Rather, it is intended to offer information to help the
reader cooperate with physicians and health-care providers in a mutual quest for optimal
well-being. We advise readers to carefully review and understand the ideas presented and
to seek the advice of a qualified professional before attempting to use them.

Published 2024

Cover and book design by Charli Barnes
Alebrije folk art sculpture by Gaspar Calvo and Nayeli Cruz

Printed in the United States of America

BK06809

Library of Congress Cataloging-in-Publication Data

Names: Celidwen, Yuria, author.
Title: Flourishing kin : Indigenous wisdom for collective well-being / Yuria
    Celidwen, PhD.
Description: Boulder, CO : Sounds True, Inc., 2024. | Includes bibliographical
    references.
Identifiers: LCCN 2024016443 (print) | LCCN 2024016444 (ebook) | ISBN
    9781649632043 (trade paperback) | ISBN 9781649632050 (ebook)
Subjects: LCSH: Well-being. | Indigenous peoples. | Ethnoscience. |
    Ethnopsychology.
Classification: LCC HN25 .C43 2024 (print) | LCC HN25 (ebook)
    | DDC 305.8--dc23/eng/20240628
LC record available at https://lccn.loc.gov/2024016443
LC ebook record available at https://lccn.loc.gov/2024016444

Contents

Yu'un Te Lum K'inale viii

Dedicating x

Petitioning xi

Reverencing xii

Introduction: Watering Flourishing Kin 1

Some Critical Notes 11

Part 1: Contemplating

Chapter 1: Ancestors of Earth and Bones 25

Chapter 2: Contemplation as Truth 37

Chapter 3: Flourishing as Connection 51

Part 2: Reverencing

Chapter 4: Indigenous Peoples and Reverence in Action 65

Chapter 5: Epistemological Equity by Elevating Indigenous Sciences . . 71

Chapter 6: Intergenerational Trauma and Intergenerational Bliss . . . 85

Part 3: Collecting Well-Being

Chapter 7: Kin Relationality 105

Chapter 8: Body Seed 117

Chapter 9: Senshine 133

Chapter 10: Heartful Wisdom 153

Chapter 11: Ecological Belonging 163

Chapter 12: Reparations Through Right Relationships 181

Reemerging. 197

Glossary 202

Notes 205

Recommended Resources by Yuria Celidwen 228

About the Author 233

Practices

On Practicing 28

Stories and Lands 31

A Spiral Path 43

Truth and Connection 56

Reverencing Home 96

Kin Relationality 112

Body Seed 127

Senshine 146

Heartful Wisdom 157

Ecological Belonging 174

Seedlings of the Earth 193

Reemerging 199

To listen to these practices, follow the link
yuriacelidwen.com or the QR code:

Yu'un Te Lum K'inale

Wocol awalik yu'un telabai bekón te'jkopé, yu'un te taleshé

Ja kich' ta muk' te lum k'inal
yu'un kuxineletik Nahua, Maya, sok xučyun Ohlone te banti ayone.

Ja kich' ta muk' stalel skuxlejal
te sbabi jme' jtatike sok ja kich' ta muk' skuxinelik
te mach'a kuxinemikixe, te ya'tike,
sok spajel chabeje
te banti ya spastik k'in swenta k'ulejaltike
sok lekil kuxlejaltike.

Yakalotik ta beel ta pojelbajtik
yu'un te jme' tatike
te lok'emik ta nutsel ta slum sk'inalike.
Ya jnatik te maba tik'
a te ya kich'tik biltesel sok naelbajtike.

Yatik ya jletik ya'telinel kuxinel.
Ta swenta te ayik ta uninele.
Ayinel ta k'inal: jlum k'inaltik,
jlum k'inaltik ta jpisiltik,
banti jpisiltik yu'un te lum k'inale.

Belonging to Earth

Thank you for your presence and attention to my voice. I strive for it to resound in your heart as a Relative. I bow to the Lands of the Nahua and Maya Peoples of my Ancestors and the Lands of the Xučyun Ohlone Tribes where I write.

I invite you to gather in respect to the traditions of our Elders and Ancestors of water, fire, blood, and bone, living in the spiral of time past, present, and to come, celebrating our cultural richness and legacies.

We continue on the path of reclamation and revitalization of our Indigenous voices. Knowing that it is not enough only to acknowledge us by name, we now seek action:

> Action for Belonging
> Action for Our Mother Earth
> everyone's Mother Earth
> because we all come from
> return to
> and belong to Her

To listen to the author recite this poem in Tzeltal, follow the link yuriacelidwen.com or the QR code that appears on the table of contents.

Dedicating

To our Ancestors, All our Relations, and our stories.
To the Siblings of my heart.
To Mother Earth, Water, Sun, and Skies

To you
I am forever grateful.
Blinded by your light, I learn to walk in the dark
and vow to serve all Sibling souls in our shared path.

I recognize You, Mother Earth, with Your presence and guiding voice
representing all directions in the vastness of our relations
as Our Kin.

I wholeheartedly acknowledge my human and more-than-human Relatives
displaced and dispossessed of territories and identities.

May we all find home.
Honoring the rightful stewards of the Lands
Bowing to the Elders past, present, and still to emerge
Weaving trust with our planetary Relatives
Celebrating Spirit

Petitioning

Asking permission from the source of Life
from our selfless Mother Earth
the very roots of Our Kin
whom we call Our Mother

Asking permission from our Ancestors
returning to the Lands becoming nourishment
to our caretakers, loving partners,
and all others we welcome as Our Kin

Asking permission from our great Spirit
our sacred maize and our cacao
and all our Relatives
embodied and in subtle realms

Asking permission from all beings and phenomena
two-legged, four-legged, finned, winged, myceliated,
rooted, flowing, and still,
in the waking, dream, and cosmic spheres

Present
knowing our challenges are deep
may our shared way onward
be kindness and compassion
collaboration and action
through reverencing, respecting, responding,
reckoning, repairing, rematriating,
restoring, reconciling, and reemerging
for Mother Earth and Spirit
for Love

Reverencing

I bow to Mother Earth and all Her grounds diverse where I find kin.

I am grateful to three of them for offering me the imaginal warmth
of a home in belonging. In them, I have grown roots throughout
an otherwise nomadic life. While still occupied today, these Lands
continue to bring life. Likewise, may the Indigenous Relatives
removed from them continue to reemerge as kin inside all hearts.

The seed Land of my birth and early years is Coelhá, the
Wonderlands of Flowing Waters, in the highlands of Chiapas,
Mexico. It is the home to the most extensive biodiversity in Mexico.
It is also North America's last remnant of cloud forest, now under
threat of disappearing by 2050 due to climate emergencies. Coelhá
sat in the municipality with the most Maya speakers in Chiapas:
the Maya Tzeltal, Tsotsil, Ch'ol, Tojolabal, Zoque, Chuj, Kanjobal,
Mam, Jacalteco, Mochó Kakchiquel, and Lacandon.

The island of Manahatta is in the Lenapehoking Lands of the Lenni
Lenape Nation, the "Original People" in the Unami language. Most
of our Lenape Relatives were forcibly removed from what is now
New York to Oklahoma under the Indian Removal Act of 1830. Still,
their soil bears their flesh and bones. Today, Queens is the most
linguistically diverse borough in the world, where its people speak
over 800 languages. Home to the United Nations Headquarters, the
island was the home of my professional work defending the rights
of Indigenous Peoples and Mother Earth for almost two decades.

The Lands of the Xučyun Confederated Villages of Lisjan is one
of the many Ohlone Nations in the East Bay Area, even though
the Xučyun still struggle to get federal recognition. Berkeley was

home to the 1964 Free Speech movement and was the first to adopt Indigenous Peoples Day in 1990. These Lands are a new home for my research and praxis of belonging and bridging in service of Indigenous Relatives worldwide through the University of California, Berkeley.

Introduction

Watering Flourishing Kin

WE LIVE IN a time of biocultural crises.[1] The growth of interest in global flourishing and environmental stewardship speaks to our need for collaborative partnerships to find solutions to repair the damage done to Mother Earth, more-than-human Relatives, marginalized groups, each other, and ourselves.

This critical moment impels actions of spiritual urgency. It implores the pursuit of collective well-being and flourishing kin for all living beings and phenomena on our shared home planet.

How would it be to care for Grandfather Fire, for example? Or to listen attentively to Grandmother Water and her chants of rain? Or even, I dare you, to hold the rage of Grandfather Lightning?

Seeking to flourish is a universal tendency in the fabric of all beings and their cultures. In this book, I encourage you to consider that a sense of flourishing *claims* us collectively.

Flourishing is a gradual unfolding of aesthetic arrest, a succession of awe-induced palpitations of stillness of the mind and embodied effervescence. Flourishing brings the realization of belonging and thus manifests reverence for life and the pursuit of creative action for the well-being of the planetary community.

In its many forms, contemplative practice opens these strings of progress as we wander through trails of intentional experience.

Attentive presence unleashes varieties of transformation and spiritual experiences throughout these trails.

While the paths may seem daunting, messy, or overgrown, the practice both grounds and lightens us, and the journey opens us to transcend our limitations of identity. These limitations are the labels about ourselves and others that have become reified, so thick they make us stuck. We have forgotten that we once created these identity stories, and because of their very nature, they can be retold to set us free. My life's journey and work have centered on this possibility, and I have found both helpful hints and some quicksand hindrances.

The elephant in the room—or blue whale in the shrine—of contemplation is science's focus on serving Western goals of individual well-being (and capital). That is, the modern pursuit of health and happiness has centered on human flourishing.

Contemplative science's most famous iteration, the mindfulness movement, has identified many health benefits, especially stress reduction and cardiovascular health. However, this Western paradigm has overlooked the concept of *collective flourishing*, which is front and center in Indigenous traditions.

Indigenous contemplative insights from traditions worldwide offer approaches that differ from the Western paradigm in significant ways. Indigenous core focus is relationships over individual experience, the sacred and spiritual over the secular, and cultural expressions such as rituals, storytelling, and ceremonies over metrics, transactions, and utilitarianism.

Indigenous contemplative sciences were absent from Western studies on the science of flourishing, happiness, and well-being interventions until my work pushed for this presence about a decade ago, pioneering the introduction of Indigenous forms of contemplation into the field. This first-of-its-kind book begins to fill that gap by drawing upon my scholarship, storytelling, and practices from the world's Indigenous traditions and their millenarian ecological, social, and spiritual knowledge.

I have come to see these values as *principles for collective belonging*. I trust these ways of being are our proven pathways to collective planetary flourishing kin. These principles explore the diverse lifeways of Indigenous traditions around the globe and how moral ethics may bridge Indigenous and Western knowledge systems to address our collective planetary aspiration for health, wellness, justice, and equity for living beings and the environment.

Mindfulness is probably the most common type of contemplative practice known in the West. The mindfulness movement bases its research and conventions on Western secularized translations (often male) of Eastern traditions, particularly Hinduism and Buddhism. The benefits of these interpretations have been studied predominantly on WEIRD groups—an acronym for Western, Educated, Industrialized, Rich, and of Democratic origin.[2] Likewise, these mindfulness practices have been made available mainly to White privileged audiences.

When imported from other cultures, contemplative approaches can lose the collectivist motivation and ethical pursuit of source traditions, often developing condescending narratives.[3] There is the risk of spiritual bypassing, spiritual consumerism, extractivism, capitalization of traditional practices, and the corporatization of spiritual traditions.[4] This kind of appropriation perpetuates patterns of cognitive imperialism, racial injustice, and inequality.[5] Alas, this bias renders Western contemplative science colonial in origin.

Furthermore, the study of contemplative practice has yet to fully explore how we interact and function to benefit the collective; how we develop a sense of community, social ethics and justice, sustainability, and a commitment to ecological restoration; and how it cultivates the experience of the sacred and spirituality. Recent attention to practices focusing on compassion, loving-kindness, and service reflect this growing need.

My activist and academic work aims to contribute to mending this oversight. I have centered my research on the nature-based contemplative practices inspired by Indigenous traditions of the world, in reverence for the planet and as a practice of spirituality. My life experiences urge me to break the patterns of exclusion and uniformity (of traditions, target populations, focus, and benefits) of the current paradigm.

Perhaps you have felt this is an urgent concern, too. Perhaps this is what moved you to pick up this book. Maybe you believe, as I do, that contemplation constitutes a wide variety of ontologies and epistemologies—ways of being and knowing—including practices and experiences that are divergent from each other and vary in characteristics, purposes, and aspirations.

In the past, the infusion of cultural diversity in Hinduism, Buddhism, Daoism, and Abrahamic traditions positively shaped our Western globalized culture. I am confident that revitalizing Indigenous sciences will move us toward a new planetary identity story. We will further enrich the scope and inspiration of constructs and reemerge as an empowered plurality, one of social and environmental transformation toward collective flourishing.

Indigenous traditions are the most diverse repository of wisdom regarding *kin relationality* (the vast web of relationships within a welcoming environment) and *ecological belonging* (our shared responsibility to all beings in our Mother Earth system).[6] These Indigenous traditions are at the forefront of the movement for planetary health and environmental restoration and conservation. Given the crises of loneliness, the climate emergency, and the imperiling of biocultural diversity, the time could not be better to reorient the contemplative paths from human happiness toward these principles of collective flourishing.

Why Me

As an Indigenous woman born and raised in a marginalized community, who has studied in public and private institutions through scholarships, worked in the private and public sectors, and lived in international settings, I have navigated diverse social groups. I soon realized that othering is much larger than my single story.

Othering is the fruit of well-established and supported systems. We, the othered, suffer from abuses and assaults of all sorts on our souls, minds, and bodies. Spiritual, psychological, emotional, sexual, and physical violence, as well as discrimination, exploitation, and tokenization are our daily bread. We grow thick armor and learn to survive with the othering worms digging underneath our skin.

The magnitude and complexity of these conditions call for spiritual reckoning and responsibility of action.

There is such enormous dissonance between the realities lived by all of us who have been othered and the flow and kinship Mother Earth grants readily.

I was born and raised in what I fondly call my forest in the clouds, in the highlands of Chiapas, in Mexico. Contemplative living has been my vehicle for making sense of, articulating, and reclaiming my "indigeneity" (my identity as an Indigenous person). It is also what drives my scholarship. These pursuits allow me to integrate ethical and spiritual ideals into everyday life from a perspective that aligns with the rights of living beings and the revitalization of Indigenous wisdom for reverence of Mother Earth. My calling joins with the global collective efforts of the Indigenous movement to reclaim public platforms to promote community care.

It is Mother Earth who calls upon all communities to reclaim the dignity and respect seized from Her hundreds of years ago.

For the past fifteen years, my professional career at the United Nations has supported the defense of the rights of Indigenous Peoples and the rights of Nature, pushing the international community to commit politically to what our Earth community demands. These seeds have bloomed into my thesis on the principles of collective well-being, the exploration of how kin relationality elicits the experience of responsibility for ecological belonging. This inquiry is focused on identity formation, as well as the practice and experience of transcendence, understood broadly as the ability to enter into a direct experience of kin relationality that manifests as prosocial behaviors such as compassion, ethics, and a sense of awe, love, and sacredness for all life. It is the innermost secret of belonging, presence, and flow.

Ultimately, I aim to cultivate a world where flourishing kin emerges as the fresh greenery of life, where every voice has a home and purpose.

Who This Book Is For

This book is for you who are eager for a world of flourishing and kindness for all. Perhaps you are a health-care professional, psychologist, therapist, human-resources professional, or digital mental-health provider looking to create meaning and belonging at home and in the workplace. Or maybe you're a wellness community worker, yoga instructor, life coach, meditation practitioner, or student engaging in the science of human happiness, mental health, environmental studies, ethnic studies, health and wellness, or mindfulness practices. No matter what has brought you here, you likely share an interest in the ways of happiness, flourishing, environmental restoration, conservation, and sustainability. Perhaps you have started to feel that some of these fields and the actions related to them are not quite meeting your expectations. Perhaps you have even felt disillusioned with how many of these ideals are being carried out or oriented by policy decision-makers. Most likely, you are yearning for change but do not quite know where or how to start or what your role and responsibility are around all of these fields. I can't wait for us all to learn more together.

What's In This Book

Indigenous populations have achieved a sense of well-being for millennia despite acute threats to our cultural and social communities and environmental conditions. *Flourishing Kin* shows how this remarkable adaptive resiliency offers feasible solutions to today's collective challenges: the climate crises and related anxiety, the social and health inequalities exacerbated by the COVID-19 pandemic, the mental health epidemics of loneliness and hopelessness, and the social and environmental demands for diversity, equity, and justice.

Flourishing Kin draws upon and synthesizes glimpses of the wealth of the world's Indigenous wisdom with Western scientific insights on flourishing. It shows how Indigenous perspectives experience the essential acts of flourishing centered on all beings and the collective WE that is our planet.

This book highlights the distinctiveness of Indigenous contemplative traditions and presents some of their ecological practices critical to sustainable collective well-being. These practices are the seeds of collective well-being and of a spiritual and relational reverence for Nature. *Flourishing Kin* explains how we can use this ethos to address our widespread ailments, from health and environmental crises to the ongoing harm caused by colonial systems, to create a new story of interdependence, reciprocity, and ecological responsibility.

The contemplative practices in this book are inclusive, diverse, and respectful of the source Indigenous traditions and lineage holders. I have gathered these practices through my innovative translation and distillation approach of epistemological equity that bridges Indigenous and Western sciences. The latest robust and interdisciplinary scholarship supports this book, updating and significantly expanding the cultural, social, biological, and neuroscientific understandings of flourishing.

Flourishing Kin gives voice to my Indigenous lineages. My Indigenous upbringing, lifelong inquiry into my heritage, practice of contemplation, and professional career have given me a unique perspective based on community and Indigenous environmental stewardship. My constellation of life experiences sets this book apart from the crowded bookshelves of the wellness industry. As a result, much of this knowledge may be new and even challenging to you—in its content and in its conveyed nature.

And so, I will guide you along these trails of flourishing by fostering insight, participation, and creation of a place of belonging. At the same time, I believe you will find comfort in how Indigenous forms of contemplation converse with and complement other contemplative traditions.

Moving beyond what you might know about contemplation, mindfulness, stress, happiness, and flourishing, I invite you to journey with me through *Flourishing Kin* with your heart on Mother Earth. To entice you into this journey, I outline how this book will empower your human capacity for connection, belonging to the larger Earth system, and becoming an agent of reemergence.

Part 1: Contemplating

As we commonly do in Indigenous traditions, Mother Earth is the first to welcome you into the collective story. She lets Her voice speak through my home and lineages and the images, metaphors, stories, and wisdom of my background. A few of my core formative experiences illustrate my lifelong inquiry into inclusion, connection, and belonging. These stories elucidate how life experiences drive our sense of meaning.

I introduce the Indigenous spiral of contemplation, which spurs virtuous motion along its path by a deliberate aspiration toward awareness and ethics. I show how the trail of the spiral path leads us to meaning within the body, heart, mind, and spirit to a merging with the collective and the natural world. Together, we will traverse life's natural cycles and polarities: dynamic yet poised, careful yet bold, challenging yet familiar, grounded in the now and consistently returning home . . . transformed.

Part 2: Reverencing

This section looks at the emerging trends around the beliefs and customs of Indigenous Peoples. It explains why the great diversity of the five thousand Indigenous Peoples of the world of varied places, contexts, habits, traditions, and beliefs cannot be singularly defined nor studied through a single lens. I deliberate on how Indigenous and Western epistemologies differ from and complement each other beyond the usually simplified notion of collectivist vs. individualist. I show how Indigenous knowledge systems break from the current science of human flourishing, which centers on the human being. I explore the Indigenous ethos of flourishing kin, whereby happiness lies within the individual's responsibility to the flourishing of the ecosystem. I invite you to journey with me through my life's work, which synthesizes Indigenous and Western sciences to offer a plural and comprehensive resource for the collective flourishing of all beings and Mother Earth.

The words *Indigenous, autochthone, aboriginal, Amerindian, First Nations,* and so on are designations of a political category built on the religious oppression and othering of colonialism. We will explore how the traditions of Indigenous Peoples are, by definition, connected to the political aspect of colonialism and the ongoing detrimental consequences known as coloniality. As a result, jurisprudence derived from those tenets harmfully impacts access to all forms of equity—from self-determination to international legal frameworks, religious freedom and violence, sovereignty and governance, and land rights and environmental stewardship.

Language is an instrument of power because it defines identities. As such, we will discern how language represents our individual and collective sense of reality and how it establishes the connections between those convictions. We will also identify the power struggles arising from language and create a shared understanding of why it is imperative to learn how to respectfully approach Indigenous Peoples' calls for equity in all ways of being, learning, and relating.

Part 3: Collecting Well-Being

The heart of *Flourishing Kin* is cultivating an insightful, collective, practice-based, flexible identity. As such, storytelling, cultural tradition, and other forms of enhanced contemplative practice like rituals and aesthetics support our journey through this section. The following principles are the seeds we will be watering to let our sense of kin flourish:

Kin Relationality is our ability to perceive all living beings as Relatives—a perspective shared by Indigenous Peoples worldwide.

Body Seed explores the body as a vessel of experience and as the root connecting us to a sense of place and our shared Lands around the globe.

Senshine, a playful coming together of *senses* and *sunshine,* looks at how we use all of our senses—heart, belonging, safety, dreaming, imagination, memory, reason, sound, sight, touch, smell, and taste—to brighten our experience of life. It nurtures the observation of direct experience as a source of traditional wisdom.

Heartfelt Wisdom focuses on the power of emotions to orient our skillful action for planetary flourishing. Here, storytelling compels positive, other-focused emotions like reverence, gratitude, compassion, kindness, awe, and moral beauty. These transcendent emotions enhance prosocial behaviors for our flourishing kin's sustainable, collective well-being.

Ecological Belonging renews our awareness of being part of the extensive Earth system. Thus, it elicits a commitment to revere Mother Earth. This sense of devotion raises nature-based contemplation and narratives of belonging.

Reparations Through Right Relationships offers engaged practices that raise pathways of reparation, restoration, and the return of benefits to Mother Earth for life's generous and vibrant diversity, and to Indigenous Peoples. The ethical principles and recommendations laid out here guide the reparations for ongoing injuries related to the use of Indigenous wisdom, Lands, medicines, and traditions. These applied ethics honor Indigenous origins and suggest ways to return benefits that support Indigenous flourishing.

Reemerging

Reemerging is the first rotation of *Flourishing Kin* throughout the spiral path of collective well-being. It is the everlasting story of our contemplative skills returning once again to the observation, embodiment, narrative, and reflection of shared experience. It reminds us that obstacles will invariably appear, yet the gradual path moves like a spiral. This symbol recaps life as ever-changing and returning. It is reminiscent of continuous progress that keeps returning home to a familiar place, yet never meeting on the same ground. It is an homage to our continuous transformation and reemerging.

You will find a glossary of terms and a resources section at the back of the book should you be interested in a deeper dive into my work on Indigenous contemplative sciences. You will also find links to audio versions of each practice in the book.

I believe *Flourishing Kin* will offer you and our culture at large a more integrated approach to flourishing, one oriented toward collective well-being and the health of our planet. By bridging Indigenous sciences and their millennia-old relational, contemplative, and ecological insights with Western scientific findings, I hope to inspire you to lead your communities as agents of reverence and reemergence, promoting flourishing for all kin and our shared Mother Earth.

Some Critical Notes

BEFORE DIVING INTO the pages of this work, some critical notes will significantly help me orient you toward Indigenous worldviews. I hope these notes begin to build better bridges between our ways of knowing and aid you in getting a little bit more familiar with my writing position. Some of these notes may sound introductory. Setting a beginner's mind is intentional. The beginner's mindset is a most helpful place to incite curiosity. You will find in these notes various topics, from Indigenous languages, the plurality of Indigenous Peoples, respect for traditional protocols, and Free, Prior, and Informed Consent (FPIC) to the now ubiquitous yet mostly lackluster Land Acknowledgments. May these initial orientations invite you to enter feeling welcome, just as I hope you would feel coming to a newly met Relative's home.

On Indigenous Languages

At the beginning of every speaking engagement or here in the Invitation to Enter *Flourishing Kin*, the audience often listens to my introduction in my Indigenous language. While I have Maya ancestry on my father's side and Nahua Tlaxcalteca and Ñañhu Otomí on my mother's side, I grew up in the Maya area of the Ba'tsil k'op Peoples (the People of Truth), known in Spanish as Tzeltal. Thus, this is the language I mostly heard as a child and the one I feel most familiar with.

In the Invitation of this book, you will find a taste of the writing in what we call our original language, Ba'tsil K'op, the True Word, or Maya Tzeltal language. If you use the QR code, you can listen to how this language sounds in the recording of my reciting it. This opening with the Native language that I heard as a child is an invitation to entrain the resonance the language has in my heart.

Apart from being a statement of presence, speaking my Mother tongue invites you to come forth to listen to sounds that may be unfamiliar. It is not surprising these Native languages haven't been commonly listened to. Historically, Indigenous languages have been silenced for centuries due to colonialism. You may have heard that boarding schools prohibited children from speaking their Native languages so that the children would acquire mainstream languages. This happened to me. I was discriminated against for speaking my tongue and was advised against speaking it in public for fear of jeopardizing the possibility of social mobility.

It is troublesome yet inspiring to comprehend how crucial this statement of presence is. Let me explain a bit what I mean by this, from the particular to the universal aspects of language preservation.

There are thirty recognized languages in the Maya family of Mesoamerica. Around 6 million people speak one of these Maya languages in Mexico and Guatemala—eight are spoken in the former and twenty-one in the latter. Tzeltal is one of these.

I have listened to Ancestors on my father's side speak in Tzeltal since I was born. Because of family migrations from Guatemala to Mexico, I have Ancestors ascending from my Grandfather speaking Mochó, Mam, and Kaqchikel Maya. My Grandmother's line has lived for the nine generations we know of in the Chiapas Ocosingo Valley, speaking Tzeltal and Spanish.

Estimates from the 2020 census suggest that 590 thousand people are monolingual speakers of Tzeltal. Together with Tzotzil (550,000 speakers) and Ch'ol (130,000 speakers), these three are the only Maya languages that are flourishing—due to recent revitalization initiatives to slow the cultural loss and recover linguistic diversity. Most other Maya languages are endangered, and two have become extinct.

Another example of the diversity of Indigenous languages is from the Nahua Peoples, Ancestors on my mother's side. The Nahua are the largest and most diverse Indigenous group in Mesoamerica. The Nahuatl language originates from the Uto-Aztecan language family and has more than twenty variants.[1] Before the Spanish colonization, the Nahua were composed of various groups sharing practices, beliefs, customs, and linguistic aspects. The ancient Nahua tribes split off from other

Uto-Aztecan-speaking peoples and migrated from the current Mexican states of Durango and Nayarit to central Mexico around 500 CE.[2]

In the fifteenth century, before contact with Spain, a collection of Nahua ethnic groups lived in and around the basin of what is now Mexico. The more influential of them formed a political coalition called the Triple Alliance in 1427, nearly a century before the Spanish arrival. This Alliance brought together the city-states of Tenochtitlan (Mexica, most commonly yet erroneously known as Aztec, Nation), Texcoco (Acolhua Nation), and Tlacopan (Tepanec Nation). The Mexica nation may be the most famous, but they were the last group to arrive in the area and become dominant due to their war-driven nature.

The Nahua continues to expand southward from Mexico to Guatemala, El Salvador, Honduras, and Nicaragua.[3] While 1.7 million people self-identify as Nahua in Mexico today, many speak mutually unintelligible variants.[4]

I recall my Elders reaching out to Mother Earth and our more-than-human Relatives in these tongues. My Grandparents, Aunties, and Uncles spoke them, however, less and less as time passed. We started talking in Tzeltal only among the community, then in private. The stigma of speaking an Indigenous language carried identity wounds from which colonial society forced us to hide. We were encouraged to learn the settler-colonial languages to guarantee social mobility. Others, in turn, distanced themselves from the tongues, trying to assimilate, adapt, and conform to the ideals—twisted as they are—of mainstream structures.

Those were other times.

Those were times of banishment and falling.

Those were times of shame and hiding when colonialism and its practices of discrimination pushed for only a handful of languages.

We are losing complex webs of relating, naming, experiencing, learning, and being day by day. These ecological complexities are dissolving like our planet's glaciers.

In a way, languages maintain and respect the equilibrium of these natural flows because they nourish Spirit and give it a voice. When the tongues of Mother Earth fade—wordings as diverse as her landscapes and Peoples—it also dwindles her living presence. We forget how and when She speaks to us. We forget Her ways of gratitude and reverence. We disconnect from Her web of relations. We deny our responsibility to and impact on others. As a result, we unknowingly block our path to the flow of flourishing.

And so, in time, even Mother Earth hid Her Spirit from us.

Many humans didn't realize when we started speaking only to other humans. Eventually, most fell enamored with the sound of their own voices.

But times are changing.

As resistance is relentless, so is cohesion.

Times are changing as water shifts, enlivening those she touches—or drowning them.

Like water, enraging, receding, and returning in full force, Indigenous languages resurface in tides of cultural restoration.

Like water, Indigenous wisdom persuades the rock heart to yield.

So, too, I believe humans are relearning how to listen.

By bringing our sounds to the people, we breathe new life into our cultures and ways of being. We conceive our places, origins, and nourishment through a spiral time, enduring our stories to the present.

We are committed to preserving our intangible heritage, emotions, thoughts, art, and spiritual expressions through our languages. We remember that the health of languages relates to the health of the people and the planet, and that collective states of flourishing and well-being are the rivers of living systems within natural cycles, emanating a sinuous grace in their surroundings.

Over half of the 6,700 languages spoken today are Indigenous (almost 4,000). While Nahuatl and Maya Tzeltal seem to be healthy living languages, recent estimates have shown that half of the world's Indigenous languages are spoken by less than 1,000 people, resulting in the loss of one Indigenous language every two weeks. I shudder at the stark projection of 90 percent of all Indigenous languages being lost by 2100.

The Los Pinos Declaration was signed in Mexico to highlight this critical language loss. It calls for the Decade for Indigenous Languages (2022–2032), inciting the international community to join Indigenous

Peoples in urging for the integration, preservation, revitalization, and promotion of our multilingual tongues and linguistic diversity at the local and global levels.

The first University for Indigenous Languages launched in Mexico in 2023 with the mandate to ensure mother tongue, bilingual, and multilingual education. Worldwide, many actions are sprouting to guarantee access to health care in Indigenous languages and to strengthen our Indigenous medicine systems. Initiatives are establishing justice systems, public services, and policies in our Native languages. Promoting Indigenous knowledge is happening in technologies and media in our languages.

By honoring these different voices throughout time and space into the here and now, we incite awareness and action. A sudden insight, moment of wisdom, commitment, and hope bridges identities with possibilities and opportunities for becoming kin.

Exquisite treasure chests that open up cultures, knowledges, and ways of being, languages are the sound practices of our Ancestors' lifeways. They remind us of how they experienced Lands and life. We learn to care and belong from these songs because we have become familiar with them. We have made them family, we have made them kin.

As the conduit of new stories, languages are creators and destructors of worlds. Their performative quality extends our circle of care for Mother Earth.

The Tzeltal poem that begins this book sings of our living lifeways. It is a bittersweet song of diversity and planetary health to reverse biocultural loss. It is a challenge to the ongoing human othering of colonialism. It is a call to action to keep singing life through these sound windows of values and cultivate hearts to reclaim their place and belonging.

It is the song of a world in which children do not need to hide. A world in which we listen to our Ancestors of Earth and blood right here—in the whisper of these pages and out there in the plazas, in the markets, and why not, also in the digital worlds.

It is the lullaby of the grandma to her grandchild, who is dreaming while awake.

On the Plurality of Indigenous Peoples

To speak about Indigenous Peoples is to discuss plurality, diversity, and ceaseless change. Living, dynamic Indigenous cultures are tremendously complex to explain in a cultural overview. This book considers certain agreements on Indigenous identities and shared worldviews that have helped establish an international collective voice. However, these insights do not intend to be comprehensive or speak for those voices represented unless through their own stories.

Indigenous Peoples represent around 6 percent of the world's population and live within the most culturally diverse and enduring traditions.[5] And yet, across these nearly 5,000 cultures, we share similar perspectives about relationality and caring for Mother Earth.[6] The mere capitalization of the words "Land" and "Country" emphasizes the cultural importance and vital relation with our Landscapes.

It is well known that Indigenous Lands make up a third of Land-protected areas, containing almost 80 percent of the remaining biodiversity now harshly threatened by the climate crisis.[7] Furthermore, Indigenous Peoples all over, as widely diverse in tribal identity as the biodiversity of our territories, are threatened by exclusionary practices of colonialism and coloniality. Therefore, for Indigenous Nations, nourishing strong relationships, reclaiming our Lands, and ensuring the conservation of Mother Nature are matters of survival.

The Indigenous movement has found consistency within plurality and unity by asserting symbols that allow Indigenous Peoples to emerge as political actors in the international community. Our agreements on a global identity have been intentional with the sole purpose of constructing a global movement that rises above multiethnic differences to create assemblies, consensual processes, and platforms of participation in the international, regional, and national political arenas around the world.

However, the right to self-determination also grants each Indigenous Nation the right to define their customs and traditions. Self-determination is one of the most vital demands of justice and presence. It is a way to get past historical discrimination and marginalization in national and international political and judicial frameworks. The emergence of this robust global influence has been called Indigenous diplomacy, which moves through the international community through horizontal and democratic structures.[8]

On Respect for Traditional Protocols

Indigenous traditions have endured ongoing appropriation, exploitation, extraction, capitalization, and commodification of tangible (e.g., material property) and intangible heritage (e.g., intellectual property, cultural skills, traditions, arts, rituals, ceremonies, and genetic material) by Western research with devastating consequences. My life's work with my Indigenous lineage and other Indigenous traditions follows strict protocols for proper and respectful approach, translation, and dissemination. I work closely with traditional Elders and knowledge-holders to identify the most relevant practices of their region to be shared with the world for planetary benefit without infringing on what is culturally sensitive. Oral traditions and knowledges have only been shared with the Elders' approval. Together, we orient this research toward a new generation of collaborative work on equal standing with the West. We are keenly aware of ethical principles of acknowledgment, knowledge-translation, benefit-sharing, and belonging.

My mother, grandmother, great-grandmother, and so on were Spirit medicine practitioners. My father, grandfather, great-grandfather, and so forth were poets (poetry is a medicine for the soul). I have faced the push for assimilation for my entire education in Western systems. Fortunately, my lyrical and medicinal lineage roots are rebels and have held firm. As you will see, my Indigenous ontology and epistemology invariably appear in my expression. Some of my stylistic choices will seem unfamiliar, even incorrect, to non-Indigenous readers. I ask you to question the role that a Western-biased mindset of linguistic coloniality may be playing in such interpretations.

Among the style differences you will notice are purposeful capitalization to denote respect and awareness of personhood (e.g., Mother

Earth, Lands, Ancestors, and Indigenous Peoples); the use of collectives and plurals to indicate multiplicity and plurality (e.g., of our wisdom, sciences, knowledges, Peoples, Lands, etc.); the use of Indigenous names in favor of colonial names (e.g., Turtle Island for North America, Abya Yala for Latin America, and Indigenous-specific tribal names instead of settler-colonialist identifications).

I generally avoid the use of pan-Indigenous language. It only appears when applied to the global political identity and shared issues that have achieved consensus agreements (e.g., working definitions within international entities, policies, movements, and so on). This attitude is part of a robust movement toward the Indigenous reclamation of identity aimed at asserting agency, difference, and plurality. We transform prejudice by bridging and educating on what it means to be Indigenous.

On Free, Prior, and Informed Consent (FPIC)

Indigenous Peoples assert our tangible and intangible intellectual cultures. The mere idea of property is a Western notion of ownership from which many Indigenous traditions distance themselves. Being Indigenous does not ever imply the loose handling of cultural wisdom or other Indigenous oral traditions. As a stand against extractivism and appropriation, any material constituting Indigenous cultural property will clearly state their lineage holders and will be used only under appropriate permission.

Indigenous cultural property such as traditional knowledges and oral traditions follow specific protocols for their use, sharing, and implementation that require permission from lineage holders. Any stories, ceremonies, and rituals shared here have been granted permission for respectful sharing with a wider audience. No cultural property whatsoever is shared that is deemed sacred and intended only for traditional member-specific use.

We are here.

We stand strong.

We are changing the world.

With the purpose of replacing the stereotypical views, assumptions, and generalizations about Indigenous Peoples, this book offers a glimpse of the sophistication, current standing, living and adapting, and transformative power of diverse Indigenous perspectives on living.

On Land Acknowledgments

Land acknowledgments have become ubiquitous today. Institutions have a disclaimer recognizing that they have historically benefited from the Indigenous Peoples and Lands on which they stand without returning the benefits to the original inhabitants. Acknowledging is the first step. Now, institutional transformation through community engagement is the next imperative step. Reparations are urgent. Recognition of Indigenous governance is essential.

We must move from an identity of othering to one of belonging. We must do so in a way that honors Indigenous presence, dignity, and reemergence. Institutions must begin to establish relationships that return Lands and benefits to their original stewards, restoring authority, recognizing Indigenous Tribes as Nations, and establishing kinship.

That is to say that naming is not enough.

Land acknowledgments are not enough.

Collective action rises as far as collective insight happens, with a vision for humane societies and institutions based on flourishing kin. Engaged relationships center on reflection and reorientation through reckoning, reparation, and revitalization of lifeways that pursue planetary flourishing.

What do Indigenous worldviews or *cosmovisions* tell us about how to do this? What do they say about who we are and the community-created identity versus the self-created one imposed upon us? How do we learn to relate based on narratives of belonging? How do we connect intentionally and compassionately with the larger Mother Earth community?

Acknowledgment may lead to flourishing as long as it translates into action that ensures access to education, health, safety, and overall dignified living. For our Lands, this means protecting their personhood, thus the rights to the well-being of waters, forests, soils, and skies.

Land acknowledgment is a starting point, but there is much more in terms of reparations that must be done. Demand that your institutions participate in the restoration of dignity and home for all. Some explicit and recognizable initiatives are free education and scholarships for Native students, from elementary school to earning a college degree; Indigenous representation in tenure-track faculty positions; institutional Indigenous-led review boards for all concerns related to Indigenous affairs; and, of course, LandBack recommends ways to return actual Land and initiatives to restore authority to Indigenous stewardship and Land management. Some of these ethical ways to right relationships will be covered here, and we can create more possibilities together.

PART 1

Contemplating

THESE WORDS ARISE from willing my full suspension of disbelief.

Finding home has been a lifelong challenge for me, and, therefore, a constant source of inquiry.

I grew up hearing persisting narratives of inadequacy and doubt imposed upon me by a classist, racist, patriarchal, heteronormative, colonialist society glorifying Spanish heritage. It has been an equally long journey to shake those stories off from crawling underneath my skin.

Perhaps that is why dreaming comes naturally to us othered.

> Dreaming is the chrysalis of hope
> where time without time is unleashed
> where we set ourselves free.
> In the face of impossibility,
> we realize we can fly.

On my migratory routes, I have been seeking the voices of the holy, flourishing kin by sharing stories of meaning and the nature of reality. I landed in the emerging fields of contemplative studies and science, where I knew I belonged. Or *wished*, I should say, because in my early days, nearly two decades ago, I felt I didn't quite fit. It was a familiar reaction, having been a misfit from childhood, with my one wing in the wilderness and the other in the magical realism of Indigenous culture. So, when nobody looked like me or spoke of the songs I heard in childhood, I did what I have always done: I rebelled. Not for confrontation but because these songs are way greater than myself. And when their stories hold truth, they resonate like a silver bowl.

Still, very few willingly hold space for such songs—especially when the songs carry burning truth. So, I persist, insist, and persevere, only to find time and again dismissal, discrimination, rejection, mockery, push for assimilation, extraction, exploitation, and many other horror stories. Still, I keep getting up, if only just a tad more bruised.

Such an elusive art to point out the water to the fish!

In a sea of myriad voices—lucid, well-versed, articulate—mine felt too raw. But then again, my voice goes well beyond the single seed. It comes from and goes back to our Ancestors, our Lands, our Mother Earth. It is Her one voice that sings to the seed about the forest, that incites the spark into the wildfire.

Contemplation *is* our shared home.

Impermanence recalls dynamic natural cycles. Kin relationality echoes emptiness. Conciliation nurtures coherence. This is a life choice, relentlessly questioning what we sense and how we perceive and then appraise. It allows us to compost old stories and sow the seeds of new, shared ones.

Yes, we carry intergenerational trauma
and *also* intergenerational bliss.

So, I write these words rooted and embodied yet dreaming we can fly. May we keep this *home* that cares to listen, question, and in the utmost gentleness, respond.

1

Ancestors of Earth and Bones

I GREW UP in El Paraiso Coelhá, the Wonderlands of Flowing Waters, in the heart of the cloud forest of Ocosingo, Chiapas—Mexico's southernmost state. Coelhá was three quarter parts forest, maize, and coffee beans, and one-quarter dreams. During the day, the Sun released a scent of moistened glory, lucid greening, and effervescent dynamism. It was the time for action and expansion. Nighttime was more subtle. Soothing. Moonlight was calmer. It was the time for the mysteries and the stories.

> Why do I speak in the past tense when
> I know spiral time is now?

My lineage voices *are* liquid chants of water. Entire realms sprout from their songs. Grandfather, Wolf of the Oak Grove, instructs endlessly to the legion of cousins to sow, plow, carve, forge, cut, clean, brush, scrub, tidy, organize. Grandmother, Trail in the Sky, nourishes the legion-now-turned-seedpod with wonders of our kin and myths of light and shadows.

> Their intimate and expansive senses are fluid, almost elemental.

> Father Skies pours boundless horizons on the mountaintops.
> Mother Earth welcomes the dim-lit
> chambers where the kernels rest.

As medicine people, my Relatives and I have our hearts in the fundamentals. We caress the skin of Mother Earth with bare feet, gentle step by gentle step. We embrace transience with carefree grace since we are well acquainted with the secrecies of order and disarray, the wholesome tension of creation.

Hence, I always say that my lineage holds the gift of balance. My parents receive it from their parents, who obtain it from their grandparents, who get it from their grandmothers, who grow it from the very roots of Mother Earth. We welcome both rosy-fingered dawns and storms the same. We listen to the wisdom of Elder trees, the chants of the wind, the whims of seasons' breaks, the gossip of the birds. We tend to Mother Earth with the kindest care, as should be done with a dwelling made—indeed—of Ancestors.

My bloodland and bloodline rest in those forests in the clouds.

The forests and the skies bear a fondness.
They are feral playgrounds for awe and frolic in freedom.
The woven roots shield the wombs that hold
the vast expanse of potentiality.

These forests are succumbing to the rising burning temperatures. But the threats of fires, gusts, and floods have not silenced their streams. Not yet. Fiercely, streams of greenery still carry my Elders' songs. My heart still sings these memories today.

Forests reveal how decaying matter gives way to new life forms. Fungi—master alchemists—break down structures into granular constituents. Then Spirit reconstructs these primary particles in myriad waves. Transformation is the act of surrendering to Spirit, the animating principle of life.

The epiphanies of interdependence with local ecosystems enact the guidance of our Ancestors. We revisit traditional knowledge and practice right relationships. Through the Ancestors' stories, we gather directions on stewarding Lands, cultures, and worlds.

My Elders initiated me into breaking loose from the grip of concerns—the graceful art of turning arrest to action, then sublimation. I sail the tides into the beautiful pitch blackness of Mother Earth and open to the vast brightness of the Skies.

Every night, enthralled in my lucid woodland quest, I sense my verges break. I become the softest moss and whisper river songs.

In the forestland, amidst the starlit whole, earthen caves, and their stories, I discover resilience, patience, and the lissome meaning of flourishing. I awake to the contemplative life.

The forest in the clouds nourishes my insight with a deep love of relations at the core of Mother Earth. She rises, decays, and returns with her tale of movement, change, and belonging. Tender seedlings whirl like dancing mystics to the Sun. Perhaps to reach the center of the world—the primordial tree that bows with its roots reaching the pitch darkest realms of the Underworld and opens her broadest canopy to the vastness above.

From Nature's kindness come beings of Spirit, beings of Love.

The same spiritual wandering has driven me on global pilgrimages to meet the atypical voices of the holy—from the fierce yet gentle warmth of the "untouchable" to the devotion of the gang member, the redemption of the inmate, the monastic perseverance, and the renunciate. In these voices, I find kin. Some of these are sacred traditions disguised. They are cells that become dolmens, where identities turn to dust and liberation is attained.

Amidst kin, Relatives mirror each other, time and time again.
We resonate.
We know one another before sharing our stories.
We break bread.
We take time to dwell in and welcome the eyes of one and all.
We revel and share joy and loss.
We embrace the same grief, dreams, and hopes.

From beginningless times, the winds of awe within—beyond—tease the many ways of will and sense, churning chaos into form. The cosmic force rises in constant flux and in full limerence incites beginningless encounters with ancestral time.

The whole Skies open.
The full Moon glares.
Fire in the wild burns all trace of grief.
Stars surge out of our eyes,
breaking the banks of bondage.
What has passed and what is to come is now.
Our Ancestors in each of our beings and breaths.
They meet us here.
They have always been present.
Their wisdom is our actions.

On Practicing

Flourishing Kin is intended to be a book held within the heart, body, mind, and Spirit. By this I mean that it is not a book of ideas. It is a book of stories, emotions, perceptions, sensations, and all sorts of invitations to sense, dream, dance, sing, imagine together.

The practices in this book are invitations to shared experiences of creation. They aim at steering you toward what may be called "shared sacred spaces." I may be guiding and accompanying the journey, but it is you who is willing to open those spaces for us to enter together.

The openings in each practice are not locations or positions but states in the emotional heart. The spaces should feel safe to explore even when they may seem unfamiliar. While little-known, they should be enthralling enough that they incite curiosity and rouse the chills of cherished treasures.

These treasures are memories once known but long forgotten, suspended in the vastness of marvels. They are secrecies defying explanations yet remarkably known in our bodies. The shared sacred spaces lay, therefore, within silent awe before the mysteries of life.

These practices take the path of dialectical examination, memory, and insight. They invite you to examine how you relate and how you perceive your relationships. Mind that there are tremendous differences between (a) merely looking at an object, (b) analyzing how we relate to it as a subject, and (c) what impact we have on each other. The inquiry of these practices invites you to work on these three aspects through an inquisitive conversation.

In these practices, I guide you by virtue of paths of exploration through memories and stories. Keep in mind that stories are created. There is one or many makers involved. After them come many more storytellers who add a bit of their own dramatist talents. In oral tradition, stories evolve and are always changing, depending on the storyteller and the listener. Stories are never still nor come in one single version.

The practices in *Flourishing Kin* break the pattern of understanding contemplation as a first-person practice that is purely self-reflective, stationary, and static. That is, I will orient you into including the Indigenous intersubjective power of second-person dynamic action and interaction.

Overall, the practices are twofold. On the one hand, they are experiential, as we will sit presently in inner exploration and mentally picturing. On the other hand, the practices are explorative, as they animate you to follow the intuitive inner exploration into an interactive story weaving with others. This entails learning about the experience of others. In other words, engage with the stories with their makers and tellers, the Lands' own inhabitants, out in the Lands themselves.

We will explore the power of stories more deeply through practice, gradually approaching sitting and listening to other voices through our memories and dialogues.

After our memory explorations, we will go on the lookout for the Lands' own voices and their stories.

At the end of each chapter, you will find a practice to help you integrate the concepts and notions laid out in it. I encourage you to take these practices seriously and go over them several times. You may find that with each round you go deeper into what eventually will be a carefully crafted story of yourself. Perhaps, at one point, you will find that parts of that story are ready to be let go of and new lines will appear.

As you will notice throughout the practices, every place either indoors or outdoors, surrounded with others or alone, is perfect for practicing.

However, to avoid the rigidity that comes with attaching to a comfortable place, the different practices will invite you to explore different places to carry out the practices. Initially, it is pertinent that you find places that feel safe to you. Do not push yourself to explore areas that feel edgy. Gradually, you will learn to find ease in unexplored places and rest in stillness and dynamism in the enthusiasm of curiosity.

As you travel through the cherished treasures that are these practices, pay attention to the emanating stories about yourself, others, and the world that will be rising in your mind. Be aware that many of them are engrained in mainstream narratives imposed upon all of us by social structures that allow only particular versions of reality to remain at the forefront. Remain attentive. Do not judge, shame, or take blame. Just observe what these stories are telling you about yourself and the world. Keep a critical eye of inquiry and a trusting heart of curiosity. By listening to the stories, they start losing their grip, and eventually they will dissolve under scrutiny. Then, the seeds of new stories will sprout.

May these new narratives flourish with all the world as Our Kin.

In the Quest for Insight

Each practice offers a quest for insights, a few cues to further reflection. Let these cues animate your experience. Feel each of them as they rise in the body, heart, mind, memory, imagination, and belonging. Let them simmer. Let what connects you to the world emerge.

A Contemplative Treasure Chest

I highly recommend starting a contemplative journal. Jot your responses to the quests for insight in this chest of cherished treasures. Imagine it to be your trusted friend, a companion through your explorations. Note these coming investigations as a stream of consciousness in your explorations of heart, body, mind, and Spirit. Let what comes be free of judgment. Let your expressions be perfectly imperfect. Let whatever is coming rise freely.

It is helpful to articulate your experience in any way you wish, whether through words, drawings, colors, collages, song, dance, or any expressive way that gives voice to your contemplative journey.

Make it playful.

Give it a name, even!

PRACTICE

Stories and Lands

Welcome to the stories of Our Lands, the circle of care that contain the collective bonds nourishing your life. In this practice, we approach each bond as a root in an intricate web that makes your world a shared world. Each root has a distinct color, tone, sensation, emotion, form, imagination. We invoke upon each of these roots to continue to strengthen your landscape. Moreover, we will come to know how to start reciprocating them for their support, strength, and nourishment.

Pause

If you haven't done so already, turn off your devices or leave them in a different place from where you will do this practice. Find a place within easy reach where you may feel comfortable. If this place allows you to overlook the landscape, that is fantastic. If you can sit outside surrounded by the natural landscape, even better. Wherever you decide to sit, make it easy for you, so your practice becomes accessible whenever and wherever in your daily life.

Let your body rest in a way that helps you stay relaxed but attentive. While you may know that some meditation practices engage in contemplation with eyes closed, in this practice you keep your gaze soft, taking in your surroundings with a panoramic view.

Pause

Notice where your attention is.
Notice.
Who, where, when, how . . . is your mind wandering?
Notice.

Gather your attention
gently
and bring it back to this present place and moment.

Request permission to enter the Lands.
Offer your gratitude for their welcoming.
Open.

Breath

Anchor

Presence

Notice the texture of the Lands where you are.
What are the smells, fragrances, scents
forms, colors, and shades
tones
sounds, resonances, timbres
rhythms
touch, temperature, strokes
tastes
memories
imaginations
breath.

Acknowledge

Recognize

Welcome

Welcome to the Lands
Welcome the Lands

Pause

Who
What
Where
are The Lands?

Pause

The Lands tell stories.
They have voices.
They sing songs.

Pause

With the utmost care,
as you would to a precious Elder or a newborn child,
pause
to listen

What are the Lands telling you
right now?

What are they saying about themselves?

What are they saying about you?

Pause

Take a few moments to hold the experience.
Embrace our first opening into our shared sacred space.
Offer your gratitude to the space for opening to and welcoming you.

Take a few deep breaths.

Now, let the experience go.

In the Quest for Insight

As a reminder, each practice offers a quest for insight, a few cues to further reflection and elicit discernment. Let these cues animate your experience. Feel each of them as they rise in the body, heart, mind, memory, imagination, and belonging. Let them simmer. Let what connects you to the world emerge.

- How are the Lands connecting with you?

- What are their languages?

- What forms, smells, sounds, tastes, textures, memories, come to meet you?

- How do they arise in images, sensations, emotions, sense of safety and belonging?

- How do you relate to what rose in this interaction with the Lands surrounding you?

A Contemplative Treasure Chest

Jot the responses to the quests for insight in your "journal-chest" of cherished treasures. Remember to imagine it to be your trusted friend, a companion throughout your explorations. Note what rises as a stream of consciousness in your explorations. Let what is coming be free of judgment. Let your expressions be perfectly imperfect. Let whatever is coming rise freely.

Have you given your journal-chest a name? By doing this, you personalize these conversations with your journal, as if continuing the considerations with a trusted companion.

Try to articulate your experience in the language you prefer, and explore different ways of expression, whether through words, drawings, colors, collages, song, dance, or any form that gives voice to your contemplative journey.

Make it playful.

To listen to this practice, follow the link yuriacelidwen.com
or the QR code on the table of contents.

2

Contemplation as Truth

MY MAYA ANCESTORS would say that one key to flourishing is to embrace the swaying and vagaries of life. It is an art to rest in the unknown. It takes grace to trust the pacing of the days, at times endless, at times radical. Holding the unfolding requires the courage to surrender to the turning and returning of the cycles.

Flourishing and resilience are closely connected. Both voice a call for adaptation to the ebb and flow of events. They encourage us to be creative in generating resources. They urge us to shift perspectives, especially from victimization to empowerment, and from power to humility.

We oscillate dramatically, like a yielding pendulum submissive to life's apparent polarities until we reach the insight of plurality. Worldviews based on our connection to natural cycles prompt us to open to a progressive spiral of becoming. This spiral is the path of going and returning through the contemplation of dynamic yet poised, careful yet bold, and challenging yet familiar ways.

These reflections are foundational to what can be considered Indigenous *cosmovisions* or perceptions of the universe as worldviews. These outlooks about the world attempt to make meaning of the interactions and relationships occurring among living beings and phenomena in all their contextual configurations.

The cosmos, or order of the world, manifests in all expressions of knowledge—medicine, ecology, the arts, and all forms of interaction. Creative and destructive natural forces are considered impossible to control, but humans stop resisting their presence and open to their influence through ritual. As such, the workings of the universe guide human practice and participation in the larger community.

Affirming a cosmic identity that considers the workings of the universe requires us to venture into the vast mysteries. Multiple nuances of how the world unfolds design a complex landscape. To give them a name, then, is to acknowledge these nuances. We experience life with heightened granularity. We move from oversimplification and essentialization to a unified plurality. One that is many times impossible to measure and explain.

In defining Indigenous cosmovisions, we encounter significant challenges. We find that global, regional, and local relationships are not linear. Our lifeways are deeply intertwined with our ecosystems, spirituality, cultural systems, social customs, institutions, political identities, jurisprudence, governance, and so forth. Naming these lifeways impacts our identities and right to self-determination. To define distinct perceptions through a universal lens results in granting power and resources—political and otherwise—to mainstream categories and their metrics over Indigenous contextual views.

To reclaim our power, current Indigenous cosmovisions have returned to language that reasserts our belief systems. For example, *Abya Yala* means "Fertile Land," "Vibrant Land," and "Flourishing Land." It is the name given by the Guna Peoples of Panama and Colombia to the territories known as Latin America and the Caribbean. The name Abya Yala has been adopted by Indigenous Peoples of Latin America as an identity nomenclature reclaiming our collective territories. Similarly, Turtle Island is the common name used to refer to the Lands known as North America.

For non-Indigenous readers who may be unfamiliar with the use of these terms, it is worth clarifying that adopting and normalizing the preferred Indigenous nomenclature is an acceptable way of supporting Indigenous Nations right to self-determination. It is also a way to honor the distinctive characteristic of Indigenous Peoples to be named after the chosen terminology in their respective Indigenous language. As mentioned earlier, the term *Indigenous,* while vital for political reasons, has the downside of unifying and generalizing particular contexts.

Indigenous principles are intricately related to the Lands we steward. These values come from millennia of observing Nature. It is astonishing and inspiring to find within these complex systems a common theme in the perception of the world as a nourishing and at times devouring mother. The mother image reflects the same swaying and vagaries of life. She embodies the turning and returning of cycles.

The multifaceted mother character guards us from the childish narcissism of expecting an eternal provider. It also keeps us keenly aware of the ever-changing nature of events. Most origin stories and creation myths speak of the destruction of previous eras as a punishment for moral ugliness. For example, there are plenty of stories in which water destroys the world. The Nahua *Leyenda de los Soles* tells of eras ending in cataclysms. The Diné cosmology *Diné Bahane'* narrates the journey of humans through different worlds. Most of these creation stories speak of eras coming to an end due to the loss of a sense of sacredness and ethical behavior. At the same time, the stories tell of a cyclic return, with a new opportunity for reemergence.

Cosmogonic worldviews—the conceptions of the world's origins—explain the generative aspects of life. They are embodiments of the living systems of Mother Earth and relatedly of our spirituality. The many ways these graceful patterns work have been the focus of Indigenous sciences in the form of storytelling, ritual, and ceremonial expressions. For example, while Indigenous Nations in Abya Yala have distinct spiritualities connected to their culture and landscapes, it is possible to observe similarities in perceiving flourishing, health, and well-being as the strength that comes from cultivating connection, caring interactions with living beings, and enhancing the conservation and restoration of ecosystems. These ways of relating ensure planetary health and the honoring of Spirit. They manifest themselves in a continuous, thriving life for all.

The worldview of the spiral path frequently appears in these communities of Mesoamerica and all along Abya Yala. The spiral path is the path of the sun, snake, or snail that describes how phenomena unfold as in a spiral. This coiled cycle is a metaphor referring to a nonlinear, ever-changing path of continuous growth. The trail expands and contracts, departing and returning to a seeming beginning point, yet remaining distant from it even if almost unperceivably.

The spiral path contrasts with the Western idea of linearity that goes from birth to development, reproduction, and death, while meeting societal expectations about achievement and status along the way. The most obvious analogy to the spiral may be cosmic cycles, especially those of the moon and the sun through calendric systems.

As an example of these lifeways, to this day Mesoamerican Peoples, most notably the Nahua Mexica and the Maya, keep a keen eye on cosmological cycles through astronomical and contemplative observation. In practice, this means examining sophisticated astronomical motion systems through a 360-day solar calendar (called *xiuhpōhualli*, from Nahuatl *xihuitl* + *pōhualli* = year count) and a 260-day lunar calendar (called *tonalpōhualli*, from Nahuatl *tonal* + *pōhualli* = light count), understood as the count of days. While these calendric systems are similar since the Nahua calendar was developed from the much more ancient Maya system, they differ in orientation and in the specific influences and deities that orient the energies of the days.

The most salient similarity these calendars share is how both orient our relationships with the planet and the cosmos through daily energetic influences and motions. The moon and the sun draw paths as they liven the coming together of the Skies and Mother Earth. The sacred calendric systems are divided in groups of *trecenas* (thirteen days) and *veintenas* (twenty months) of influences called *naguales* (archetypal energies). These pairings change over the year, never falling on the exact same day as days in the Gregorian calendar. The path of these calendars is one of a spiral, indicating seasonal changes, ceremonial observations called *xukulen*, and ritual practice. The energetic influences of the months and *naguales* dictate medicine, Traditional Ecological Knowledge (TEK), and all relationships and interactions, human and otherwise.

Along those lines, the Maya spiritual guides called *Ajq-ijab* are the keepers of time who as traditional medicine practitioners carry the *Pison Q'Ajq'al*, a sacred wrapping and medicine bag containing the red seeds of a tree considered sacred and used in ceremonial and medicinal practices since precolonial times. These seeds signify the *naguales* of the calendric cycles. The many groups under the umbrella terms of the Maya and Nahua Peoples of Mesoamerica use these seeds as instruments for counting and observing the influence of the web of life and its rotations, as well as for divination practices orienting human action in daily life. These seeds also have medicinal anesthetic properties and are used to protect from disturbing influences.

Another example of nonlinear cycles is the commonly known "medicine wheel" used by several plains tribes on Turtle Island. It is worth noting that this name is a Western one, so these ceremonial sites should be referred to with the names designated by the Native Nation based on their distinct relationship with their ritual spiritual systems. The most ancient of these archeological sites is in the Bighorn National Forest and it is called *Annáshisee*, or "Large campsite," by the Crow Nation where it stands. The Crow Nation, however, has noted that the site was already there when they arrived in the area. No other Nation has claimed ownership of it, making it possibly the most ancient of these ceremonial sites. In a nutshell, this system presents a multidimensional scheme of seven directions that indicates a web of interconnected influences radiating out from a center to a surrounding whole.

Aspects of these spiral cosmovisions also exist in our everyday perceptions of well-being and personhood. Consider that spirals never touch the same trail again, even when progress is slight and unnoticeable. Now think about the spiral nature of healing, moving through challenges while at the same time one is making sense of these experiences and finding one's place and purpose. With each turn of the cycle, or spin of the wheel, our feelings, narratives, and sense of identity are transformed. These timeless cycles reveal our innate nonlinearity. The spiral path reveals how our world is continually changing.

While obstacles invariably appear in any venture, the spiral path reminds us of how a shift in turn—even a slight one—changes perspectives. The spiral path evokes movement, shift, transition, transformation, however slight; thus, we are bound to shed our previous skin, like the snake, and leave the old-self, decaying beliefs to be composted. No matter how stuck we may feel in a situation, we are bound to reemerge.

Feeling lonely and alienated from the world may engender images of paralysis, apathy, idleness, and aimless drifting. The waves of futility carry us endlessly, not strong enough to drown us but thick enough to keep us exposed. Our minds turn their brief attention span to images of creepers, insects, clinging vines, and rancid, moldering, festering food. Suppurating wounds may populate our nightmares, crumbling down our sense of self. Yes. This is good. That old self needs to crumble. That old story needs to change.

The spiral path helps in such situations. Natural cycles of barely perceptible shifts may become sudden turns of transformation. A gradual path helps to integrate that change to keep it sustainable. You can reclaim the power of letting go of the old, festering narratives of othering, where we or others do not seem to fit. You can recondition into a new story of belonging. You restore the regenerative force of Mother Earth into your new self. The cycles become more palpable with the establishment of new stories of reparation.

> Contemplation is the art of truth.
> Mending broken threads,
> we create stories of becoming.

At its very essence, contemplation itself is a spiral path of becoming. It is an exercise in letting go of fixity. It welcomes the fluid patterns of emergence, transformation, and return through the renunciation of reified identities. We surrender to the upheavals of the heart, mind, self, and Earth by surrendering the delusions of attachment and acknowledging the truths of conciliation and universal belonging.

We reclaim the agency of our relational creativity by offering ourselves as nourishment for others. In other words, contemplation is a personal and collective spiritual experience. It is life in its full force. It is a path to becoming a spiritual being.

All times meet in the spiral path, right here, right now.

The spiral path locates us in intergenerational webs of relatedness that have been lost in our fragmented twenty-first-century living. We are connected to the roots of memory from our Lands and Elders. This is the past stretching within the spiral path.

Memories cultivate wisdom, and we attain insight from community participation. This is the present unfolding. Participation stimulates responsibility as we let the old self decay to become food for a new form of life. This is the future derived from the spiral path and orienting our intention today.

In our practice together, I hope you will feel these forms of relationality.

The responsive cosmic system involves all phenomena. Spirit weaves us into the collective web of the cosmos with its innumerable elements and beings. In that sense, the spiral path also depicts the luminous vastness in the body, the connecting of the Lands through the heart, the mind, and the plural unity with Spirit. These insights bring coherence and greater meaning to human participation in the larger Earth community. All beings are represented in the vast cosmic web of relationships as part of a responsive living system that involves all elements and phenomena.

Our hearts connect to Mother Earth through phenomena.

We will start realizing this more and more as we keep along the spiral path of contemplation, consistently returning home, transformed.

PRACTICE

A Spiral Path

This practice takes the path of belonging, memory as story, and insight. It invites you to examine how you relate to People and Lands and how you perceive your relationships with them. Move from looking at your own experience to analyzing the impact your inquiry has on both of you. Converse with what you are experiencing as a subject. Interact with your practice.

The practice is twofold. In the first part, venture into sitting in present inner exploration and mentally picturing throughout the practice. The second part incites you to follow the intuitive exploration and move to an interactive story hunt. This entails learning more about those you visit in your practice from themselves, makers and tellers. At least those you can think of as the Lands' own inhabitants, out in the Lands themselves.

We will explore the power of stories more deeply in later practices, but this is our first approach to sitting and listening to the makers' and tellers' voices through our memories. Do not expect one specific result. Let yourself be free to explore the practice and how it moves you, how it converses with you. Let the practice be a new friend you are just getting to know.

Pause

If you haven't done so already, turn off your devices or leave them in a different place.

Find a place nearby where you feel comfortable.

If the weather permits, sit outside surrounded by the natural landscape. Otherwise, choose a place that allows you to overlook the landscape.

Make your chosen place easy to access. Ideally, your practice should be accessible at any time and place in your daily life.

Let your body rest in a way that helps you stay relaxed but attentive.

Turn to eyes closed as long as it is comfortable for you. Closing your eyes will help you avoid any distractions from your senses engaging with the world. However, many of us are not yet ready to practice with our eyes closed. This may be so if we deal with a higher level of stress or lack general safety in our surroundings. Be kind to yourself, and do not push beyond what is comfortable. This is a general rule in any practice you encounter. The path should be gradual, gentle, and soothing yet encourage us to move little by little beyond our comfort zone.

Pause

We traverse a first turn of the spiral,
listening to the Lands.
We turn to them.
We return to them.
We listen to their many languages.

Attuning to their voices
offering our gratitude.
We appreciate all beings that make up our surroundings.
We acknowledge these beings supporting our life today.
We accept their places and positions
visible and invisible,
subtle and coarse,
gentle and rough.

Pause

We traverse a second turn of the spiral,
immersing roots in these familiar Lands where we feel grounded.
Our roots now delve into our tender days.
Our time tendrils travel, unearthing in our childhood Lands,
connecting time and place into our bodies, hearts, and minds.

Pause

Find a place in or around the Lands of childhood that feels safe.
From this safe place we observe our home.
Turn leisurely, observing all that is around.
Who is there?
What are they doing?
What sounds or voices do you recognize?
What do you see that you had not sensed for some time?

Pause

We traverse now a third turn of the spiral
submerging roots from your familiar Lands of childhood
to unveil our ancestral bedrock.
We reach a marrow source of primordial lava core,
connecting further blood and bone into earth, rubble, and ore.

From your Lands to our shared Ancestors' Lands
invoking
connecting
relating.

Pause

We traverse now a fourth turn of the spiral.
Now your heart branches to the Lands of those emerging.
Our young ones seeking, just like you;
hoping, just like you;
not quite finding answers to the world we live today,
just like you.

What are their Lands saying to them?
What are their Lands saying to us?

Pause

We traverse now a fifth turn of the spiral,
from our youths' Lands, we sprout to the Lands after tomorrow
to the unknown Lands of those to come,
not yet named, not yet thought of, nor imagined.
The "children of our children" commonly called,
who are still at reach for our heart, mind, and belonging.
Our line of blood becoming,
finding home.

Pause

We traverse now a sixth turn of the spiral
We now are shooting spores to the Lands beyond
to even more distant Lands, further unknown.
To those Lands apparently beyond reach,

who nonetheless receive already our decisions of today.
To those of mixed blood living in them,
who acknowledge their wholesome common kin.

Pause

Now we return to our hearts today: the seventh turn.
We are the seventh generation
to whom the rest belong,
from whom the rest become.
We ground and relate to all six cyclic turns,
and return the attention.
Here,
right now.
Observe what rises within.
What senses your body?
What moves your heart?

Pause

Pay attention to these images grounding from the seven turns.
All of them flowing.
What waters stream from these images?
Note whether uplifting or mournful echoes return.
Embrace the bittersweetness.

Pause

Return your attention to the Lands that held them all.
The Lands that we call home.
Listen to those Lands' language and their voices.
How are they orienting your purpose?

Pause

Turning to those Lands of today, childhood, Parents, Ancestors,
youth, children of our children, and beyond,
we listen to a myriad of voices
reverberating.
We embrace their places and positions
visible and invisible,
subtle and coarse,
gentle and rough.

Pause

Where are they now, in you?

Offer your gratitude to the incalculable beings
supporting your life
in these Lands.
Perhaps to this day they have been unacknowledged.
Show appreciation now.

Pause

Surrounded by these Lands and supported by these beings
you are connected to preceding and ensuing Lands
through your roots, branches, and invisible spores.
All have faced challenges;
you embrace change today for the well-being of them all.

In the Quest for Insight

As a reminder, this practice takes the path of deep examination, memory,
and insight. In the first inner visualization, you are invited to make a first
visit to time past Lands, all the way to a shared ancestral past. Perhaps
this experience gives you a novel way to be with the Lands, as subjects
with whom you interact.

This is an entry point to an inquiry into the meaning of home and story as an interactive connection. The relationship with your Lands and Peoples is grounding your story to your present.

In the explorative part of the practice, you are invited to do an outer interactive storyline. This quest for insight will guide you through a few cues to further this reflection and elicit insight into your relationship with Lands and Peoples.

Let these cues animate your experience. Feel each of them as they rise in the body, heart, mind, memory, imagination, and belonging.

Let them simmer.

Let what connects you to the world emerge. Do not stop in the quest for insight in self-reflection only. Invite a conversation with those with whom you've shared Lands as home, if that is still possible and safe for you to do. Otherwise, you can develop a deeper relationship with the Lands by learning about them and how they have changed over the years.

Engage in learning about the Lands from the Lands themselves. Then continue the conversation with others who have helped the Lands express their voices—that is, the Lands' own inhabitants, human and more-than-human.

- How do the Lands where you are today conjoin the Lands of your childhood?
- In what ways are their languages similar and in what ways different?
- Who is telling the story of these Lands?
- What is their story?
- How do all the beings of those Lands and phenomena manifest and interact with you?
- How are they now touched by your presence?

3

Flourishing as Connection

THE SPIRAL PATH of truth and connection is an approach to fostering learning though contemplation. This kind of education is one that disentangles perception from conditioning, so that we can discover reality as it is without imposing judgment that may impair an experience of novelty and scrutiny. It is a practice of seeking solutions through experimentation and process evaluation rather than relying on established conventions. Such a practice develops virtues that support relationships, resulting in flourishing kin.

In academia, *contemplative studies and sciences* are umbrella terms for the humanistic and empirical study of spiritual and secular contemplative traditions, philosophies, practices, arts, and pedagogies, such as meditation, texts, rituals, prayer, and ceremonies. The field is grounded in the careful and critical observation and assessment of experience, including what it produces (its elicitors) and what contributes to it (its determinants).

The study of contemplation has transformed into a robust field of inquiry. It has centered mostly on studying the qualities that enhance flourishing as well as the tribulations that hinder it. There has been remarkable progress in demonstrating how practices like gratitude, loving-kindness, mindfulness, intellectual humility, and awe promote dimensions of flourishing in individuals. In the last two decades, the field has made practices from mostly Buddhist contemplative traditions available to the population with significant impact on physical and psychological levels.

Contemplative studies and sciences are transforming culture. Secular practices distilled from these fields are being integrated into international organizations, government agencies, judicial systems, health-care settings, education curricula, institutions, and the workplace. I am a proud champion of contemplative programs myself. For example, in the past two decades, within the United Nations, my presentations on compassion, resilience, and well-being have been broadcasted globally to all UN duty stations. From that work, I can venture to say that components of contemplative insight were integral in conceiving the 2015 promise of the United Nations 2030 Sustainable Development Agenda with its slogan of "Leaving no one behind" and its goals of equity, health, and well-being for humans, life below waters and on lands, climate action, and collective action for sustainability.[1]

The appeal of the humanistic and scientific study of contemplation is generative and auspicious. Its current interdisciplinary approach and emphasis on well-being offer compelling avenues for solutions to our current social and environmental challenges. However, this new interdisciplinary movement, still too narrowly focused on humans, also has a meager cultural focus. It lacks diversity and representation.

Contemplative science and its practices have only represented a limited landscape of cultures and a very select variety of traditions—East Asian Buddhist practices (mainly from Tibetan and Theravada traditions), and to a much lesser degree, Hinduism, Daoism, and the Abrahamic traditions of Judaism, Islam, and Christianity. Although the field has engaged with other contemplative traditions, these studies have been scarce. In other words, the field of flourishing has left some practices behind, particularly Indigenous contemplative practices.

The field of flourishing has also been insularly focused on humans, leaving behind more-than-human and Mother Earth flourishing. For years, I have urged institutions and decision-makers to understand that, fundamentally, the sciences of flourishing and contemplation are not about human flourishing alone. It is planetary flourishing that we must turn to, a global well-being that implies and develops broader ethics and scopes that encompass the sustainability and well-being of Mother Earth and all her inhabitants.

Environmental destruction and the loss of life, the breakdown of communities, economic systems of oppression, mental health epidemics, and the struggles of substance abuse, loneliness, and depression are excruciating realities worldwide. At the same time, we are seeing advances in One Health approaches, which are unified approaches to health that recognize the interdependence between human health and the health of fungi, plants, animals, and all phenomena.[2]

Similarly, the connection between human and environmental rights is becoming more apparent. An avenue for commitment opened when the United Nations adopted a new resolution on the human right to a healthy environment in October 2021.[3] We have also seen a rise in clean energy sources and nature-based approaches to well-being. Notwithstanding, some of these approaches involve environmental impacts that need to be recognized and addressed before they are fully established and their use expanded.[4]

Under examination, even well-intentioned initiatives start showing a different pulp under the husk. Some of the most shameful land-grabbing cases in modern history have come in the name of conservation. Abya Yala, Asia, and Africa have seen Indigenous Peoples displaced from their Lands to give space to clean energy transnational corporations. For example, disgraceful luxury safaris now stand in the Lands of the Maasai, Datooga, and Hadzabe Peoples at the Ngorongoro Conservation Area in Tanzania.[5] In Mexico, Zapotec Indigenous communities are standing against wind energy farms and suffering from the division it generates in their communities.[6]

It is well-known that the 80 percent of the planet's biodiversity is in tribal territories, and growing evidence shows it is better managed by Indigenous Peoples when they have governance over their Lands.[7] Under Indigenous guidance, biodiversity is restored and also a new way of relating to the environment.

Practices of contemplation have been referred to in different ways. Hindu practitioners may be familiar with the Sanskrit term *bhāvanā*, literally "causing to become," and those practicing mindfulness may have heard the Tibetan term *gôm* (*sgom*), "to become familiar with."[8] The Hebrew term *hitbonenut* denotes a practice of introspection.[9] The Christian "centering prayer" is a known silent practice aimed at focusing on nothing else but the presence of God.[10] Islamic Sufi devotees practice a variety of contemplative forms, among them *dhikr*, remembrance or recollection of the names of the Divine; the inward *muraqaba* or *sama* involving music and dance; or the lesser known practice of *madih* poetry.[11] These terms might indicate the capacity to create perceptions (cosmovisions and worldviews), to become adept in the ways the mind habitually constructs—and reifies—these impressions, and to achieve total absorption and transcendence in connection to the Divine.

The contribution of Indigenous contemplative sciences to the fields of flourishing and contemplative studies and sciences is that they weave together and interdependently the well-being of self, others, and the natural environment. They promote a sense of belonging, interdependence, and even an intimate knowledge of the sacred. In this way, Indigenous contemplative practices develop personal self-awareness skills, social skills, and ecological skills. They provide a process for somatic, emotional, psychological, spiritual, and intercultural discovery as well as sustainable collective well-being. Perhaps the first two practices you have engaged with in *Flourishing Kin* have given you a taste of what this may mean in your own flesh and bones.

Indigenous contemplative traditions have been tested and refined for millennia for their physical, psychological, *and* environmental benefits. They offer new insights into the meaning and pathways to sustainable, collective well-being—the very problems we face today. Indigenous forms of contemplation foster connection in the form of *kin relationality*: the vast web of relationships within a welcoming environment.

The conceptual focus of kin relationality reorients us to the larger systems of relationships that humans are only one part of. Kin relationality brings equal emphasis to self and the community of living beings of Mother Earth through the piercing recognition of relational networks and how they influence each other.

Similarly, Mesoamerican contemplative traditions correlate with these terms. For example, the Maya Tzeltal verb *jolin* indicates "mind habitually" and "to conceive, remember, and imagine."[12] Likewise, the Nahuatl *teitic nenonotzaliztli* and *teitic ontemoliztli* define "inner consideration" and "deep intuitive meditation."[13] In like manner, these cases suggest looking at contemplation as a practice not only of careful observation, study, and analysis, as the Hindu and Buddhist terms may point to, but also as practices that involve the embodiment and embracement of emotion, memory, and imagination.

It is common to find in these broadly distant traditions a wide range of techniques to observe the interaction of body, heart, mind, and Spirit. Most contemplative practices—especially those popularized by the mindfulness movement—center on practices of self-observation, self-regulation, and absorption. Certainly, some practices emphasize other-focused kindness, and as the few practices listed above may elucidate, some involve collective dynamic and creative practices. However, very few keep in mind the natural world, let alone interact with it.

Nature-focused practices are those cultivated in Indigenous traditions. These forms of contemplation establish a way of inner reflection that is porous and multidirectional. Surely, the serious analysis they foster likely results in remarkable refined acumen on the nature of kin relationality, ecological belonging, and the cycles of nature. These practices bring forth intuitions that form perceptions and develop social constructs about the order of the world as sentient, relational, and capable of cognizance. From these experiences, a sense of morality orients values of reverence, responsibility, awe, love, and an intimate sense of the sacredness of life. Persistence in practicing some of these techniques will likely progress into an ethical commitment of being and action to benefit collective flourishing.

Contemplation presents us with the urgent challenge to reflect on who we are, how we got here, and what we can do to create solutions to move forward in reverence, respect, restoration, reparation, caring, and belonging. However, in a world driven by ideologies of separation, we rarely see these ethical principles in practice. The crises of climate, health, society, and spirituality demand that we ask how the arts and sciences, humanities and technology—all of our different ways of being and distinct wisdom systems—can bring us together to devise solutions for a world where all living beings flourish and thrive.

So, let me insist:
Human flourishing begins with **Mother Earth flourishing**,
wherefrom contemplation is the art of **truth**,
and flourishing the path of **connection**.

PRACTICE

Truth and Connection

This practice takes the path of contemplation as the meeting place of truth that flourishes with a deep sense of connection. We aspire to cultivate an ability to meet the here and now in a dialogue of discovery. We begin by making the present moment our acquaintance. With time, this familiar friend will tell us unexpected stories that will incessantly amaze us with their freshness.

Customarily, our past experiences lead us to label and judge our present. They help us learn from mistakes and differentiate friend from foe. However, they may also hinder our ability to connect with new experiences and fully discover them for what they are. What's more, for those of us who learned to survive adverse childhood experiences, hyper-vigilance develops into a relentless sentinel for hungry ghosts. In other words, trauma ensued as an instinctual predisposition for protection.

Think of these obstacles in the following way. When distorted lenses injure our experiences, they bleed dry before we feel their pulse. Then, without the compass of a clear understanding of our emotions, we find ourselves once again entangled in harmful situations. Our relationships shatter at our high-pitch reactivity, or we avoid any possible intimacy by escaping at first sight of anyone coming close. We are unable to trust, or we lack boundaries, or both. These once-life-shielding mechanisms become the most challenging hurdles to our most intimate desires to connect and belong.

The art of truth of contemplation aids as a balm for those open-heart wounds. Contemplation aims to discover our experience through a truthful dialogue with our surroundings. The conversation is part inquiry, part active listening. We become interested in their story, voice, song, movement, and what pours from their roots to achieve genuine connection. We let our surroundings flourish as they mean to do. We meet them as they are. We allow the connection to rise from an experience of bare truth.

The practice invites you to examine how you usually relate, how these interactions shape your perceptions, and how you may respond to the world after practicing an interaction with your environment through direct dialogue. Remember, it is a practice not merely of observation but also conversation.

Test for yourself whether your ideas about experience shift from the change in outlook. Interact with your practice, too.

As with other practices, the first part incites you to venture into present exploration and observation. The second part lets you explore the intuitive aspects of an interactive conversation with your environment by following your perceptions without labeling.

Do not expect one specific result. Let yourself be free to explore how the practice moves and transforms you.

If you haven't done so, turn off your devices or leave them in a different place.

Find a place where you feel comfortable.

Wherever you are, observe how your surroundings manifest.

Let your body rest in a way that helps you stay relaxed but attentive.

Let your eyes open with a soft gaze, taking a panoramic view.

The path should be gradual, gentle, and soothing yet encourage us to move little by little beyond our comfort zone.

Pause

Notice your surroundings with your eyes open.
Go after the forms, colors, textures.
Now after the light illuminating them.
And into the source of light itself.

Catch the moment when observation construes classification.
Stop there.

Next time, stop right before that moment.
Yes. It will take practice.

Let your attention become the light in the body,
where the breath becomes the form.
Highlight the porosity of body and breath,
conversing with the surroundings.

Breath is taken by the waves of sound.
Subtle whispers and rougher tones
become a breath of sound.
Resonance opens each pore of the body,
and we become a body of sound,
where everything belongs,
reverberating . . .

Caress each moment of bare relations.
Let each become a flourishing sharing that claims you,
carrying the curiosity of meeting someone new.
Let each connection bloom from its roots.

Meet these new friends—your surroundings—as they are.
Avoid projecting assumptions, ideas, or expectations upon them.
Deter the vultures of "sameism" from feeding off the uniqueness of the world.
No experience is the same as another.
Instead, practice candid curiosity.
Unveil the intricate subtleness of others' stories.
Only then, the echoes of color tones will reveal
the connection rising from bare truth shared.

In the Quest for Insight

As a reminder, this quest for insight will guide you through a few cues to further this reflection and elicit insight into your relationship with your perception of the world.

Let these cues animate your experience. Feel each of them as they rise in the body, heart, mind, memory, imagination, and belonging.

Let them simmer.

Let what connects you to the world emerge.

Do not stop in the quest for insight in self-reflection only but also invite a conversation with those with whom you share your life.

This practice took the path of contemplation as truth and flourishing as connection. It is meant as a conversation, not a projection of assumptions or expectations.

In the first part of the practice, you are invited to ponder how our past experiences color our perception of the world. While these colored views may be truly helpful, they can also become obstacles to our genuine relationship with the world around us.

- How does thinking about each present moment as a new acquaintance give you a novel way to approach both safe and challenging situations?

- Can you think of recent situations when assumptions about others or situations may have prevented you from meeting a new experience as a friend?

- Can meeting experience as a conversation be an entry point at an inquiry into the meaning of truth and relationships? How so?

- The inner visualization invited you to encounter each moment as a fascinating possible new friend. How did this change your relationship with your present?

To listen to this practice, follow the link yuriacelidwen.com
or the QR code on the table of contents.

PART 2

Reverencing

THE INTERNATIONAL WORKING designation for Indigenous Peoples adopted by the United Nations in 1981 affirms that "Indigenous communities, peoples and nations are those which, having a historical continuity with preinvasion and precolonial societies that developed on their territories, consider themselves distinct from other sectors of the societies now prevailing on those territories, or parts of them. They form at present nondominant sectors of society and are determined to preserve, develop, and transmit to future generations their ancestral territories, and their ethnic identity, as the basis of their continued existence as peoples, in accordance with their own cultural patterns, social institutions, and legal system."[1]

According to the previous statement, the current international working designation of Indigenous Peoples characterizes these identities as having endured historical colonization and invasion of their Lands and extraction and exploitation of their natural resources—air, water bodies (from ice to oceans), mountains and forests, and all that lives in them.[2] Despite these circumstances and the growing threats of the climate emergency, the world's five thousand Indigenous cultures have formed a resilient political coalition against human and environmental rights violations.

Although Indigenous individual and collective rights have only recently been acknowledged in 2007, Indigenous cross-cultural accord has allowed the emergence of an influential relational identity in a global community beyond just a political one.[3] These identities manifest in Indigenous psychologies distinct to each Nation and that can be understood within a framework of Indigenous relationality that we will explore more deeply in this section.

4

Indigenous Peoples
and Reverence in Action

BEFORE THE 1970S, Indigenous affairs had received very little attention in the international community. The Indigenous identity as a political movement was still in its early development.[1] Within the United Nations system, earlier motions to acknowledge the right to self-determination and governance to Indigenous Peoples as Nations were brought forward in 1957 by the International Labor Organization (ILO) in a document known as the "Convention Concerning the Protection and Integration of Indigenous and Other Tribal and Semi-Tribal Populations in Independent Countries."

It took fifteen years for the United Nations to launch a study on the problem of discrimination against Indigenous populations. The 1972 survey aimed to reach out to as many Indigenous representatives as possible to reach a consensus on who and what constitutes being "Indigenous."[2] It took ten years for the results of this study to be published, in 1982, due to the challenges that implied reaching remote Indigenous Nations.

In 1989, based on the previous 1957 document, the ILO made official the "Indigenous and Tribal Peoples Convention," or Convention No. 169 for short, the preeminent framework on Indigenous rights, conceived almost two decades before the United Nations finally established the aspirational "Declaration on the Rights of Indigenous Peoples," commonly known for its acronym UNDRIP.

At the core of UNDRIP is the validation of the inherent and inalienable right of Indigenous Peoples and Nations to self-determination, the vital proclamation that Indigenous Peoples and Nations ourselves decide how to be recognized according to our *own* perception and conception and never according to the values of dominant societies.

According to UNDRIP, no state must take, by legislation, regulations, or other means, measures that interfere with the power of Indigenous Nations to determine themselves.[3] The central characteristic that guides Indigenous identity is a historical and distinctive bond with and belonging to their distinctive Lands and Territories. This implies that Indigeneity is qualified by the historical colonization, invasion, usurpation, exploitation, and commodification of our Lands, Territories, resources, air, ice, oceans and waters, mountains, and forests.[4]

Colonization and invasion have been human constants. Groups have attacked, invaded, and colonized each other for millennia, presumably since agricultural surplus strengthened sedentary groups for territorial expansion. Colonialism occurs when one territory expands against another, claiming sovereignty over it and subjugating it under the immediate control of the ruling state. It is motivated by pursuing political and economic expansion and acquiring resources (Land, people, and raw materials).

In defining the historical period of colonialism relevant to the context of the Indigenous movement of today, I am taking into account the process of invasion from the fourteenth century onward that marked the beginning of the age of exploration. The Silk Road network of trade routes to Asia established routes connecting Europe with Asia, Persia, the Arabian Peninsula, and East Africa. European powers ambitioned to exploit further more accessible routes to the Abrahamic Holy Land through the dominance of sailing in global trade. These explorations culminated in the arrival, conquest, and colonization of territories all around the world, transforming the lives of Indigenous communities with consequences that continue to this day. This timeframe clarifies the sheer inequality that divides the world between Global North developed wealthy countries, which to this day continue to exploit the Global South developing countries for resources.

Later, after World War II, almost a third of the world's population lived in colonies. Independence movements within Indigenous territories have risen since the eighteenth century, revolting against the deep-rooted oppression and its entrenched imbalance. This dismantling process is known as decolonization and decoloniality. It refers to undoing colonialism or the claim of a formerly colonized people for independence and self-determination.

However, most often, Indigenous Peoples continue to depend on colonial assistance. At the global level, Indigenous Nations have had to borrow resources from colonial powers for development and infrastructure, resulting in a new system of debt that keeps Nations as modern enslaved peoples to their liabilities. In most countries, Indigenous Nations depend on federal budget for development. Thus, colonial powers and their economic corporations remain in domination and restraint over Indigenous Lands, Peoples, and resources.

It is estimated that the world Indigenous population is more than 476 million people, spread across over 90 countries, and representing more than 5,000 cultures.[5] Indigenous Peoples live in the 7 global geopolitical regions, based on how their ecosystems face climate change: Africa, Asia, Central and South America and the Caribbean, the Arctic (and the Russian Federation outside the Arctic), Central and Eastern Europe and Central Asia/Transcaucasia, North America, and Oceania-Pacific.[6] These regions vary from deserts, high mountain ranges and plateaus, the circumpolar circle, rainforests and jungles, coastlines, tundral, and urban areas. The division based on environmental circumstances is unique and was introduced by the global Indigenous movement.

One challenge Indigenous Peoples face is the vehement refusal from states to recognize their identity and rights, as well as the burdensome obstacles to acknowledge the authority and governance over Lands and territories. Case in point is the more than half of the world's Indigenous Peoples in Asia, who resist discrimination and neglect due to proclamations of unified nationalist identities or who flagrantly suffer persecution.[7]

Only recently did China formally recognize 55 ethnic minorities in its territory. They comprise 8 percent of the population, plus almost 1 million (836,488 persons) of other unidentified ethnic groups.[8] Above two-thirds (64 percent) of the country's territory, including the extensive Autonomous Regions of Tibet, Inner Mongolia, and Xinjiang Uyghur, is home to ethnic minorities. They allegedly enjoy equal standing under the Chinese constitution, with the right to practice their language and culture. Nonetheless, maligning assimilation programs that intrude into cultural and religious habits, customs, and transmission of languages, as well as censorship and forced sterilization procedures, are known to happen regularly.[9]

This persecution happens on every continent. The vanishment of Indigenous traditions and customs escalates under cultural genocide as Indigenous ethnic and religious minorities continue to be displaced from their Lands and pushed to assimilate. It is no surprise that Indigenous Lands and water defenders and environmental activists are at the highest risk of death globally.[10]

Indigenous Rights

Some core rights that Indigenous Peoples should enjoy are autonomy and self-determination, no discrimination, preservation of diversity, and protection of Lands, Territories, and resources. These include political, environmental, legal, economic, sociocultural, and participatory rights.[11] As mentioned earlier in the chapter, several international frameworks identify these collective rights in international law.[12]

The UNDRIP aims to raise Indigenous Peoples globally as a politically relational category among the different nations, the civil society, and the dominant states. Its central themes are those mentioned earlier but worth listing again: the right to self-determination, including autonomy to governance and legal systems; the right to acknowledgment as distinct peoples; the right to free, prior, and informed consent (FPIC); the right to be free of discrimination; and the rights to Land and resources, including the conservation, protection, use, development, and control under their own laws, traditions, and spiritual relationships with tangible and intangible heritage.

Implementing Indigenous rights remains challenging despite states adopting UNDRIP, which continues to be an aspirational document, not a legally binding one. These global frameworks do not reflect state governance and public policies, except in three countries in Latin America (Bolivia, Ecuador, and Chile), which, despite adopting such rights, continue to infringe upon Indigenous autonomy.

Colonial histories have upheld public policies of assimilation that have been difficult to undo. Latin America suffers from an imposed "mestizo" identity. North America and Oceania faced abhorrent boarding schools. Africa has confronted homogenization since the decolonization process of the 1960s. Nationalist identities debilitate Asia (Burma, China, India). These colonialist-derived policies are significant and persistent obstacles that negate the Indigenous presence and thwart any possibility of plurinational governance, usually perceived as a threat to state identities.

Indigenous rights have continued to evolve, gaining visibility, even while weathering these opposing forces. Indigenous Peoples have achieved global presence using an integrative, participatory approach, impacting states and recontextualizing free trade, especially in Latin America.[13]

Indigenous Peoples continue to protest predatory industrial development and extractivism and have risen as the forerunners in environmental management and climate resiliency.[14] The influence of the Indigenous human rights movement in the fight against climate change is multilevel and dynamic, involving cultures, traditional knowledge systems, and strategies to defend biodiversity and foster collective environmental adaptation.[15]

While Indigenous Peoples compose about 6 percent of the world's population, we make 30 percent of the world's extremely poor.[16] We also have the lowest life expectancy, in some areas up to 20 years less than our non-Indigenous counterparts.[17] The lack of legally binding frameworks that require states to prioritize a global commitment to address Indigenous Peoples, coupled with the climate crisis, intensifies the urgency of vulnerable Indigenous populations (children and youth, women and girls, people with disabilities, migrants, refugees and asylum seekers, LGBTIQ+ people, and older adults) and further hinders the possibility of fulfilling the promise of equality.[18]

As we move forward, I invite you to consider the role of the unified political identity of the Indigenous Peoples movement. Consider how the plurality of Nations acknowledges the distinct and contextual relationship of each Nation to their Lands and simultaneously underlines the commitment to a united form of power against colonial imposition.

Indigenous Peoples have slowly regained autonomy through mostly nonviolent methods, including diplomacy and negotiation, and religious rebellions energized by liberation theologies and a desire for equal rights and self-determination. Decolonization and decoloniality have a significant impact on the traditions of Indigenous Peoples.

So where is the movement of Indigenous Peoples moving toward? First and foremost, newly autonomous Peoples are developing economic sovereignty and sustainability, which they have regained by returning to ancestral spiritual traditions, resource management systems, and food sovereignty movements.

This chapter is not an easy one to digest. Now imagine how it would be to write about these realities, experience them, and carry them daily under your skin. Engaging with these uncomfortable truths requires practicing moral and political contemplations about what is just and fair.

Acknowledgment of the dark heart of the collective past is an entry point at an inquiry into what home and story are as interactive connections. The relationship with the Lands you live in, the stories of those with whom you share those Lands, and those who had their homes there but were displaced only shed light on the challenges of contemplating, comprehending, and cultivating a shared home.

5

Epistemological Equity by Elevating Indigenous Sciences

FLOURISHING KIN IS grounded in a deep commitment to epistemological equity. By this, I mean it considers both Western *and* Indigenous ways of knowing (epistemologies) based on scientific inquiry, with systematic methods of gathering evidence and assessing beliefs about social and physical reality. Both forms of knowing constitute science. As you will learn, both are established within culturally specific practices of rigorous observation, analysis, and evaluation. And both encourage and advance learning, discovery, and comprehension of the world.

Nonetheless, Indigenous and Western ways of knowing differ in context, interests, and concerns. They emerge from different soils, are cultivated by dissimilar fertilizers, and yield contrasting fruit. The methods of Indigenous and Western sciences also diverge in striking ways that can complement each other in the exploration of promising new areas of inquiry.

Western science is efficient at causation: how things work and how events occur in a practical, step-by-step process of causes and conditions. But it lacks the symbolic understanding of Indigenous sciences. As Seneca/Onondaga Elder leader Oren Lyons states, "Western science speaks of resources; Indigenous sciences speak of Relatives."[1]

Indigenous sciences explore the broad expression of symbolic interpretations of the world, based on our Peoples' connection to our Lands. In this way, Indigenous sciences are ecological in quality. They unveil the complex web of Mother Earth and consider the needs of our Lands and our community of more-than-human beings.

We will all benefit from bridging these disciplines of knowledge. But first we must decolonize our research methods. We must address the lack of representation of diverse ways of knowing in our education systems and the cognitive imperialism that allows a Western-centered understanding of the world to dominate.

As a scholar, I advocate for epistemological equity by decolonizing our ways of understanding cultural wisdom. This not-yet-mainstream approach to studying the world's Indigenous cultures may be new and challenging to grasp at first. As such, I will draw on states of being and ways of learning from Indigenous Peoples to show how they relate to Western systems of knowledge. I will guide you through my deep, culture-based scientific methodology for respectfully translating Indigenous wisdom. In the end, I hope you will come to the understanding that empirical research is a place of belonging for these ways of knowing—one that can significantly advance social change.

The Fallacy of a "Universal Truth"

During the Enlightenment Era, one of Western science's objectives was to decrease the influence of the Church in administrative aspects of the state. At the time, religious institutions dictated political power and controlled social theories of knowledge and access to education, which certainly needed to be free of dogmatic views. Given the domination and othering of the religious mainstream, this objective was sensible. Regrettably, in detaching from spiritual beliefs and rituals, the Western pursuit of knowledge missed the opportunity to preserve the capacity to fall in awe with mystery. Spirit was relegated to the domain of religion, tainted with narratives of power that were taken literally.

Western science derives its quest of curiosity and learning through observation, analysis, and the generation of hypotheses and comprehensive theories to explain and predict phenomena. Relying upon metrics, its explanations of the material world assumed that phenomena repeat continuously. Western science expresses ideas about causality through theories, hypotheses, and empirical evidence that statistical analysis evaluates and verifies. The scope is linear, cumulative, and method-based, using replicable quantitative measurement and statistically driven inferential processes.

While the Western scientific method effectively reveals central, often prevalent patterns, its frequent lack of attention to context, place, and cultural diversity is a concern. Many point to the tendency of Western science toward essentialism, also understood as the inclination toward uniformity and the assimilation of knowledge (inclusive of people and places). This knowledge system has undoubtedly made unthinkable advances in our understanding of the world. It does have a role. It is not, however, the only method of learning about the world.

The problematic presumption that knowledge acquired is culture- and value-free and ready for ownership soon gives rise to a practical, utilitarian lens that addresses the question of benefit. Economic and transactional motivations may drive empirical research, and knowledge is frequently reduced to ownership concepts like intellectual property. This framework of benefit and practicality presents tough challenges regarding Indigenous rights to tangible and intangible heritage, which are frequently not understood within the communities through such specific legal terms. Reaching consensus between essentially different ontologies is nearly impossible due to these obstacles.

Furthermore, the majority of Western scientific research is known to be carried out on WEIRD samples, which stand for Western, Educated, Industrialized, Rich, and Democratic groups.[2] Western science evolved into an imperialist sphere of influence, disseminating "universal truths" about the workings of Mother Earth and her processes as if these were inert, objectified machinery. Because of this bias, you may consider the majority of Western science to have colonial roots. The world became a production line when this learning method was accepted as the only accurate means of interpretation, explanation, and meaning-making. According to Yupiaq anthropologist Angayuqaq Oscar Kawagley, such a limited perspective on science undermines the validity of knowledge gained from years of "naturalistic observation and insight" that devalues Indigenous cultures.[3]

The idea that Western science can explain any phenomenon and use it for profit is a fallacy. These priorities narrow the scope of inquiry to production, extraction, and exploitation for consumption. Paired with religious ideas of dominance over the world, Western pragmatic approaches of dominion and control became culturally embedded with the idea that humans dominate Nature. Mother Earth was shaped, restrained, controlled, torn to pieces, ravished, raped, and left for dead.

Land-based colonialism gave way to cultural and cognitive imperialism as the main focus of coloniality. The widened scope includes religious, social, political, and economic power; sociocultural norms; and belief systems. One could contend that through Western coloniality's influence over science and religion, its imposed worldview—which replaced Indigenous methods of knowing—became accepted as the only truth throughout the rest of the world.

However, what was the theme of the silenced Indigenous stories? What fundamental knowledge did they hold? How can we retrieve them? Finally, how do we change our transactional ways of being to ones grounded in multiple truths, connection, and reverence and the feelings of deep respect, awe, and humility they engender?

Insights of Indigenous Sciences

Earlier, I mentioned Indigenous cosmovisions as the origin of our reciprocal and connection-based knowledge systems in chapter 2. These worldviews are founded on distinct languages, customs, requirements, and beliefs passed orally over generations. Our Lands and Territories are interwoven with these contextual worldviews. As you have noted in reading *Flourishing Kin*, the terms *Land, Country*, and *Territory* are frequently capitalized to emphasize the significance of the Peoples' connections to the environment. Lands shape every aspect of our lives, including our interactions and expressions of culture; medical and healing practices; social, political, and economic institutions; governance structures; ecological knowledge; and educational programs. Capitalizing terms to highlight the importance of our relationships with our natural surroundings is standard practice.[4]

In addition to bringing Indigenous perspectives to the empirical research on contemplative interventions, happiness, and flourishing, my work empirically examining the basic concepts of kin relationality and ecological belonging has demonstrated ample evidence of the influence of relationships and the benefits of nature-based contemplation on environmental well-being.

Indigenous sciences orient us on how experience arises from interdependent relationships and how to use our senses as conduits to dialogue with direct emotional experiences. Theories, cosmologies, and a deeper comprehension of the human body have resulted from these investigations of our network of relationships.[5] I have led you through practices throughout this book that allow you to start cultivating these insights on your own.

Indigenous sciences pay attention to and attempt to categorize unusual, distinct, often unrepeatable phenomena. They take observations and analyses of the world and create meaning for them through oral narratives: stories, enacted stories in rituals, habits, communal portrayals in ceremonies, governance, and even judicial ways.

These narratives are accompanied by contemplative practices, such as recognizing and identifying the conditions and impact of these stories. From this comes an emotional experience of compassion, eliciting affective, cognitive, motivational, participatory, and mutually transformative action.

I like to think of contemplation as the sharpest obsidian flint, cutting through the fog of confusion into an epiphany of discernment. Obsidian is associated with the Nahua god Tezcatlipoca, "the Smoking Mirror," who grants and retrieves the wealth of fate. Tezcatlipoca is often depicted surrounded by the twenty symbols of the holy days, wearing an obsidian flint that reflects the true nature of reality. Under its complementary transfiguration as the solar god Quetzalcoatl, Tezcatlipoca guides the path of the Sun in its daily route.

Obsidian is formed when incandescent lava with high silica and aluminum content is exposed to a rapid shift in temperature. Its acute piercing quality, which comes from the opposites of heat and cold coming together, makes it a remarkable material for knives, spearheads, arrowheads, and other cutting tools. I find that the flint is a fitting metaphor for Indigenous contemplative sciences since its sharpness coming from the conciliation of opposites breaks through to reveal truth, connection, reverence, and bliss.

Tezcatlipoca is consistently associated with darkness, the night sky, conflict, and turmoil. He holds an obsidian mirror for divination practices through which he is capable of transcendent vision, perceiving a distinct image through flawless, pitch-black smoke. The portrayal of achieving insight through confusion refutes accuracy of the idea of opposites in constant confrontation moving to separate from each other. Instead, cutting through delusion through sharp awareness, the obsidian flint advocates for an integrated presence of continual flow and adaptation to the unfolding of phenomena.

Consider this: the flint of contemplative truth dissolves the dense smoke of conditioning to reveal the essential nature of truth in the plurality of multiple parallel possibilities. The flint of flourishing connection clears the path of brushwood to let the streams of connection flow, and the flint of active reverence cuts the ego into infinite pieces to marvel in awe and humility at the vastness of life.

Indigenous sciences use nonliteral metaphors to help us become more conscious of relationships. A plethora of origin stories from all over the world convey the same message: the world was silent, empty of meaning, in stillness, and in darkness at first. There and then chaos was an infinite soup of potentiality containing all meaning, however entangled. Order is yet to come. Sense is yet to be made. Ideas yet to be discerned. Origin stories usually unfold with a disentanglement of phenomena, slowly weaving the threads of the web of life. The flint cuts through the fog and reveals the true nature of all phenomena: kin relationality gives way to all narratives of life.

In this way, symbolic language guides us toward the insightful splendor of multiple meanings and expressions of emotional experience—individually in personal life experiences and collectively as cultural accounts. No quick answer or fast fix is readily available in symbols. Their art consists of holding emotions and cutting through levels of meaning, digging into their roots to the Underworld and extending to their vast canopy in the Skies.

Indigenous Nations achieve cultural wisdom by revitalizing and transmitting Spirit wisdom from Mother Earth and the Ancestors intergenerationally and among different species to create systems of plurality. Like in dreams, the Indigenous language of Spirit bridges the psychic realms of experience into all the possibilities of our environmental relationships.

Relationality is at the core of Indigenous knowledges. It guides learning through the discovery of the multifaceted and multidirectional patterns of influence in all our relations. This distinctive trait offers a framework to understand the fundamental concerns and principles of Indigenous knowledge systems that are driving research.[6]

Bridging Indigenous and Western Sciences

Many areas of academia still do not recognize Indigenous methodologies as research. However, a movement is growing toward decolonizing methodologies of inquiry and examination to open to diverse epistemologies or ways of knowing. It is an ongoing process that takes a will to actively listen to how knowledge is achieved.

Indigenous sciences explain the world through narratives, expressed in qualitative and nonlinear ways, that observe, evaluate, and document the phenomena around us.[7] These narratives give meaning to our personal and collective responsibilities toward planetary flourishing. We may delineate these narratives into four categories: oral (storytelling), embodied (ritual), collective (ceremonies), and juridical (law and governance). These groupings reflect our relational, intersubjective, and communal ways of being as well as our contextual and place-based cultural diversity. They help us make sense of our reciprocal nature with other phenomena, as well as their sentience, distinctness, and agency.

With Indigenous sciences, the methodical learning of traditional knowledge is often achieved through the contextual and metaphoric, as expressed in narratives of the self and of the collective. These practices draw upon multigenerational experiences of space and time that are expressed in ecological knowledge of land, sea, sky, and even cosmic settings. They center on what has been called relational validity, which is the precedence given to place and to a contextual interconnectedness of human life to Lands and all other living beings.[8] Indigenous sciences center these relationships in contexts of cosmologies and sovereignty. This is why colonialism and coloniality have devastating effects on shaping knowledge, cultural identities, and relationships.

Bridging Indigenous and Western sciences must be an inclusive process of learning and knowing. It must recognize the need for decolonizing research since the Western settler-colonial lens has historically excluded and harmed Indigenous Peoples and our science. And so, I bridge Indigenous and Western sciences using empirical laboratory science tools to understand the benefits of contemplative practices through qualitative testimonies of subjective and metaphoric storytelling with quantitative measures of the physiology, psychology, and ecology of living beings. I use meticulous qualitative analysis that is grounded in Indigenous wisdom distillation and narrative transmission, as well as observation, theorizing, and testing of empirical experience and phenomena.

I wield the flint of nondual awareness to ensure equity among the knowledge systems to rethink our methods of knowledge and embrace a diversity of sciences that resist homogenization, uniformity, assimilation, and conversion. My commitment is that, working together, we will cultivate a shared, multifaceted, pluralistic sense of intentional reality seeded in stories of kinship.

The remainder of this chapter contains multiple scientific terms and concepts that I will define as necessary. I have preserved the academic nature of the following content to underscore the level of scientific rigor that has gone into my work creating a bridge between Western and Indigenous sciences, one that proves Indigenous science is an equitable and complementary source of knowledge to Western science and that respects and honors the roots and context of Indigenous wisdom.

Indigenous sciences draw on a system approach to understanding the web of life and all of its processes. It recognizes the impossibility of comprehending a phenomenon simply by observing it on its own. It warns of the futile attempt to understand any phenomenon unless we view it as an entire composite. Undoubtedly, following a single phenomenon may bring awareness of its aspects, but it narrows and essentializes it, reducing it to a fallible idea with a fundamental nature. Such a perspective doesn't consider the phenomenon's diversity and dynamism. It misses it as part of a process, its part in and influence on its environment and how the environment impacts it in return.

We can bridge this contextual understanding of the world with the formal Western objective-analytical aim of the social sciences. After all, a system that looks into the complex and dynamic workings of groups offers a broader perspective on ways of knowing and the possibilities of science and analysis. If we fail to see the plurality of relationships in our natural environments, we miss the subtleties of emergent properties and synergies. This approach is a key solution toward equity for the two knowledge systems.

To know a phenomenon through its environmental interactions means to be open to the complexity and plurality of Mother Earth and its kin relational quality. This path explores how living beings originate and are nourished from their ecosystem and how they transform and decay to become sustenance for the shared extensive networks. These more nuanced outer and inner relational processes encourage an experiential sense of belonging, an essential lookout for planetary health. This culturally sensitive knowledge-translation system of collaboration and complementarity is profoundly impactful and timely for today's challenges.

Sidenote: Indigenous worldviews consider the locus of interrelated phenomena as a collective environmental body composed of a connected multiplicity. In this model, phenomena are observed interdependently as a continuous flow. Consider the metaphor of the spiral path: nonlinear, ever-changing, and continuously growing. This flow approach extends our worldview out into the universe. Indigenous worldviews do not end at the planetary level. We go cosmic. Relatives wondering with curiosity about the universal order is a typical encounter. Everyday talk commonly ends with remarks about spiritual matters, and late-night storytelling flows with flights of awe about this primordial animating principle. The cosmic order gives way to the idea of balance between and within worlds and bodies. But to not get lost in such fantastic vastness, we will keep our journey contained and grounded at our planet's more graspable and familiar level!

Translating Indigenous Knowledge

While Indigenous populations continue to suffer stigmatization, discrimination, obstruction from political participation, and criminalization in laws, policies, and practices, we also have uniquely rich resources in our traditional systems for health, care, and recovery.[9]

Despite the extensive diversity of Indigenous traditions worldwide, there is agreement on certain aspects of the relationship to place-based ecosystems that make Indigenous knowledge critical to the social and climate crises we face today.[10] These are valuable sources of knowledge for environmental stewardship and social practices related to community building, resiliency, and well-being.

However, these knowledges are not meant to be simply merged with Western scientific findings. One is individually and universally focused and the other relational and contextual—they are not puzzle pieces that perfectly and immediately fit together.

My work synthesizing Indigenous and Western sciences honors what I call the Indigenous contemplative science of rigorous qualitative analysis. This analysis is based on observation, theorizing, the empirical testing of experience and phenomena, and the distillation and narrative transmission of knowledge via spiritual exercises. My respectful knowledge translation of Indigenous systems of being (ontologies) and of knowing (epistemologies) is sensitive to context. By design it honors the culture-level needs and sharing practices of the Indigenous knowledge source as well as the broader global-level learning needs. Taking these into account achieves both knowledge equity and the ability to scale and share practices respectfully. This deep ethnographic or culture-centered approach also significantly increases the impact of findings on and accessibility to nonscientific and non-Indigenous practitioner communities.

My careful Indigenous-led ethnographic methodology results in the curation and dissemination of valuable practices while maintaining their spiritual value and benefit. It ensures that in escalating these knowledges, they are not deprived of their contextual meaning, purpose, and focus. By prioritizing practitioners of these knowledges, I aim to ensure that knowledge translation honors their intention *and* achieves knowledge equity. This type of ethnographic research also allows us to understand how different practices from different sources are related. It reveals their similar roots in the core concepts of kin relationality and ecological belonging. It leads us to a broader characterization of Indigenous traditions, as opposed to the stereotyping that has occurred with Indigenous communities following the psychedelic renaissance (more on this in chapter 15).

Indigenous Contemplative Sciences and Collective Flourishing

Presently, Western science advances the third-person methodological approach to explore routes to knowing and being. Contemplation, on the other hand, is founded on a critical firsthand investigation that promotes discernment, learning, and evaluation of one's own experience. Critical first- and third-person approaches are acknowledged by Western contemplative studies, validating direct experience. I noted earlier in the book that the majority of contemplative practices developed in the West are geared toward cultivating affect, body awareness, mindfulness, and the ability to observe thought processes without passing judgment.

Indigenous contemplative studies introduce the distinctiveness of a second-person approach, which necessitates an understanding of relationality and intersubjective experiences within and across cultural traditions, worldviews, contexts, and communities. Through lifeways that include shared rituals, ceremonial aspects of community, and narratives, the second-person relational aspect of experience is studied. While Indigenous forms of contemplation foster similar skills like awareness, concentration, and insight, they differ with those Western secular practices in that Indigenous approaches focus on their ongoing, ever-changing relationship with the social and natural ecosystem rather than individual experience alone. This supports an Earth-based identity rather than an identity based on humans.

Most often, Indigenous Peoples view themselves as no different from Nature because they are interdependent with her. Ritual narratives facilitate an understanding of one's responsibilities and relationship to the environment and community. These principles form the basis of a mutually beneficial relationship with the natural world.[11] At the heart of Indigenous knowledge systems are a respect of natural laws, based on ethical values of gratitude, reciprocity, responsibility, and belonging.[12] These worldviews have risen as models of diversity integration promoting changes and altogether new regulatory and development frameworks based on our values of respect and reciprocity. These worldviews have been at the forefront of the movement for planetary health and environmental restoration and conservation.[13]

Individual identity is based on relationships and its belonging to groups; therefore, it is embedded in a broader social ethos. As the Indigenous approach is not solely focused on the individual experience but on relationships belonging to an ecosystem, I have argued that it shifts the core focus from an *ego* to an *eco* identity. Meanwhile, Western contemplative practices are highly individualistic and prioritize medicalized interventions that emphasize independence over interdependence. This points to the Western tendency to have more concern for individual rather than communal well-being.

Research has shown that so-called WEIRD (Western, Educated, Industrialized, Rich, and Democratic) groups suffer from a sharper sense of individualism and less attunement to their own embodied selves, others, and nature.[14] However, less privileged but collectivist communities—which describes most Indigenous Peoples—appear more responsive to others' suffering and more collaborative.[15] These findings are supported by previous research in contexts of social class differences in the expression of compassion.[16]

Recent scientific studies also speak to the promise of connection and kin relationality. It has been shown that the more deeply relational the contemplative practices (e.g., loving-kindness and gratitude), the more powerfully they produce a suite of benefits for the mind and body of self and others.[17] This new development in Western scientific approaches to happiness shows naturally how kin relationality dialogues with Western scientific findings on relationships and social interactions.

It shows how Indigenous and Western sciences complement each other and offer plural and comprehensive ways of resourcing ourselves. Their bridging reveals ways of being that bring back reverence, awaken the sacredness of life, and elicit responsibility for the world.

The obsidian flint of Indigenous contemplative practice goes beyond the initial perception, emotional response, and labeling of phenomena to cut through the deception, delusion, and confusion of self-serving dispositions that impede kin relationality. It allows us to move past the conditioned self, oblivious of its surroundings and enamored with its own navel.

If we can wield this flint in our Western practice of contemplation, we can make virtuous sense of the world and our place in it. We can address the widespread ailments from our health and environmental crises. I believe we can begin to heal the wounds caused by colonial systems with our Indigenous ethics of belonging.

The cultivation of well-being via transcendent emotions—which I explore in the next section—is central to the foundations of Indigenous science. Here, scientific methods manifest as cultural ways of knowing and being that shape origin stories, rituals, habits, law and governance, ceremonies, and lifeways. This makes studying self-transcendent emotions a long overdue opportunity to diversify the epistemologies and methods of current psychological science.

In this sense, *Flourishing Kin* bridges multiple forms of empirical, observed, firsthand evidence—from the cultural and ethnographic to the psychological and neuroscientific. In considering these different disciplines, I center (1) the deep cultural study of the role of Indigenous Peoples, their sciences, the challenges of colonialism and coloniality, and their resilience, ways of healing, and paths to bliss, and (2) recent advances in the cultural evolution and study of self-transcendent states such as compassion, gratitude, and awe and how these can be of use in the context of psychological healing and well-being.

By amplifying and centering the voices of Indigenous Peoples, *Flourishing Kin* is also part of a significant movement to bring prominence to Indigenous wisdom, knowledge systems that respond to today's systemic inequalities and climate challenges. In doing so, the science of flourishing, happiness, well-being, and contemplation is taking steps toward the reparation of historical atrocities committed against Indigenous Peoples over the past five hundred years, and whose wisdom now may be critical for the survival of life.

For more on the study of Indigenous sciences, my knowledge-translation methodology, and others' efforts to bring prominence to Indigenous sciences, please see the "Resources" section at the back of this book.

6

Intergenerational Trauma and Intergenerational Bliss

THE TRUTH, CONNECTION, AND REVERENCE you have been tending are your emotional sailing tiller and rudder. These virtues orient your course, navigating the tides of contrasting emotions. As we move forward through summarizing the atrocities against Indigenous Lands and Peoples, I ask you to hold on to the practices of contemplation, flourishing, and reverence. Integrate these values into your lifeways. Use them routinely. We continue this journey in a manner that builds bridges and fully sees others despite differences in life experiences. Beyond that, we feel and think together to find ways to repair past injuries.

Administrative structures intensify the dispossession of territories and the extraction of goods apart from the mere actions of conquest, colonization, and occupation of a place and extraction of resources.[1] Conversely, coloniality describes enduring power structures that result from colonialism but go well beyond the colonial power administrations' precise bounds.

Colonialism happens even more subtly. Other treacherous manners are much more calculating and deceitful. These are the colonization of the body, mind, beliefs, and even dreams. These sly forms of control can occur in how stories influence who belongs and how belonging happens. From how we speak, appear, and act in forms ruled by politics, religion, and the media, coloniality pushes a way of thinking that follows one truth—that of the establishment's perpetual oppression.

Collective ignorance of the dynamics of the human mind is one of the main reasons diverse cultural identities are vanishing. Behind genocide and ecocide is a state of blindness that pervades contemporary society. Our unconscious characteristics, moral and heinous, are the mind's shadows.

The shadow symbolizes the unacknowledged aspirations that shape our behavior and the sociocultural contexts from which they emerge.[2] We often perceive these idiosyncrasies and quirks in others, usually through projections, but they remain repressed or never recognized in ourselves. The destruction of the environment highlights the harm to humanity's relationship with ourselves due to the shadows commanding predatorial human thoughts, emotions, and actions.

The channels of communication with the unconscious are closed off with the loss of stories. This incomplete knowledge leads to a psychological imbalance characterized by a disjointed and dissociated identity that is unable to acknowledge its place in a system. It sees itself as separated, isolated, and atomic. Consequently, it projects its predatory and destructive tendencies onto its surroundings.

Contemplation, flourishing, and reverence can stop the automatic download of stories and identities. The sensitive heart questions our perceptions, seeking truth, genuine connection, and reverence for life. We fall in awe of the other's uniqueness and see them for who they are. To reverse this tendency, we must reclaim and reimagine our collective stories from a place of belonging.

Composting Stories

White male domination over our home planet is at the core of the Western individualist paradigm. This deluded notion that an ethnic patriarchy should govern over existence most likely emerged from culturally informed constructions of Abrahamic origin from the phrase in the book of Genesis, "to have dominion over all of existence." A narrative of devotion to a totalitarian authority encourages oppressive regimes and subjugation of Mother Earth. An elevation of humans over other living beings has resulted in centuries of exploitation of the environment.

Religious texts are not analyzed for social context very often. This failure to notice contextual references is especially problematic since we risk glossing over critical aspects of race, ethnicity, and social perceptions of place and time. The book of Genesis dates from the sixth or fifth centuries BCE. It was translated from Hebrew and Aramaic into the Greek Septuagint around the third to first centuries BCE and into the Latin *Vulgate* in the late fourth century CE. These versions are each informed by distinct sociocultural conditions—from each other and those of today. Still, those versions of the Bible are the source of most translations we know today.

Take the word referencing the first human: *Adam*. The Hebrew word is a gender-neutral noun, from *Adamah* (the biblical Hebrew: המדא), which directly translates as "ground," "earth," or "seed." In most versions of the Bible, the name has nonetheless adopted a male gender to fit a heteropatriarchal system established in early antiquity.

As colonialism and coloniality advanced Abrahamic religious thought and Roman political systems, Indigenous belief systems were banned, mocked, dismissed, and almost lost to massive cultural genocide. The Abrahamic snake-loathing mythology replaced the wisdom-centered Native ways of knowing. The evil snake of Genesis was projected onto principal Indigenous cosmological deities. The Feathered Serpent, representing the wisdom of spiritual transformation, was banished from its Indigenous *Tamoanchan* paradise. The serpent went from being a symbol of awareness to one of deviance and despisement. Conscious awareness fell from the skies and turned into the wicked snake to be buried under a fallen tree.

As local mythologies and their origin stories hid under religious conversion, a disconnection between humans and Mother Earth followed. Extraction, dominion over, and abuse of the Lands and living beings led to the oppression, disempowerment, and subjugation of Indigenous Peoples worldwide.

What a loss! We lost the possibility of collective awakening and replaced it with a journey into the Underworld!

In transitioning through such a challenging journey, we can make sense of it as a transcendent experience. What do I mean by that? For example, let's look at the Mayan creation story Popol Vuh. According to the story, the Ahawab, or Lords of Xibalbá—Land of the Dead—were enraged by the boisterous ball games the divine twins Hun Hunahpú and Vucub Hunahpú played. Such was their anger that the Lords challenged the Twins to a ball game of life and death. After a long journey through all sorts of torments, the Twins arrived at Xibalbá, were finally crushed by the Lords, and perished. The Twins' sons, however, the gods Hunahpú and Ixbalanqué, who had been born in the underworld, looked for reparations. Ixbalanqué decapitated his brother Hunahpú and then gave him back his head to revive him. The Lords thought this was funny and asked to learn the magic trick. The Twins tricked the Lords into letting themselves be decapitated but did not return their heads, thus defeating the evil beings and allowing the creation of a new world.

This Underworld journey is metaphorically similar to others in various cultures despite geographies and historical periods. These stories voice a prominent human transition through states of disarray (a duel between life and death). Restoration is a process of reemerging (in the Maya story, the sons of the defeated Twins are the new seeds of change). The momentous transformation of identity results in a new form of life that gives new meaning to one's life purpose (in the Popol Vuh, the world as we know it today was created, no less!).

I venture to say that we live in one such process collectively. Our current underworld journey is akin to a global underworld journey or *nekyia*. I prefer the latter term because it implies an invocation to the Ancestors for guidance on ethical action. The concept of nekyia may include any journey of the afterlife, a descent to the abodes of the dead, or any interaction between the living and the dead.

In the nekyia, the realization of vulnerability prompts a dissolution of the sense of identity that refuses to change. These mindscapes communicate through transcendent experiences such as contemplation, dreaming, aesthetic arrests, and creative processes and can be eerily similar to brilliance, genius, or psychosis.

Names for the journey of transition are countless. The most common are the Dark World, the Night of the Soul, Night-Sea Journey, the Descent to Hades, the Belly of the Whale, and many others, but all indicate a loss of control. This humus state of transition forces life to let go, die, and decompose. Although terrifying, this dissolution is beneficial and bestows an opportunity for radical transformation. The ability to transform our perception of reality can change chaos into cosmos and confusion into order. It is an action-oriented movement toward awareness. Its goal is the restoration and integration of the whole.

While this new state of awareness may bring feelings of guilt, rage, and powerlessness, it also has the potential to prompt a process of inquiry and trigger a transcendent experience. Indeed, one enters the Underworld powerless. The ecstatic experience calls for the divestiture of any remaining aspect of identity.

As the nekyia journey devolves, one sheds layer after layer of identity until nothing remains except the bare truth. It is a process of *mythopoiesis,* or creating a new identification narrative. A new story based on the contemplative qualities of truth, connection, and reverence ruptures the previous delusion of separation and the grandiosity of domination. An earth-based symbolism of decay and renovation guides the cycles of life into collective flourishing. It is the moment of truth, connection, and reverence.

I see the planetary emergency as a psychic and organic global nekyia between imminent death and spiritual awakening. We are at a point where collective action needs to transition from self-destruction to reverence. This tension is the creative pull for collective awakening. The increase in mental disturbances is related to the destruction of our environmental ecology. The disconnection from our inner and embodied experience further detaches us from the larger community.

Genocide and Dehumanization

Our disconnection from our lived reality keeps us even more apart from society and fosters the growth of dehumanizing ideologies that drive the community away. Such is the frightening origin of the most heinous horrors committed by humans onto other humans and our planet.

The critical social theory of sovereign power and its figure of *homo sacer,* developed by the Italian philosopher, literary critic, and theologian

Giorgio Agamben, offers a persuasive argument on the separation process from Indigenous ways of being since colonial times. He based his theory on two core Western paradigms for political structures that promote totalitarian states.[3]

Agamben maintained that *zoe*, or "bare life," is life objectified to an animal state and devoid of legal protection. In contrast to *zoe* is *bios*, the so-called "good life," or what Aristotle argued legitimized social life with a say in the decision-making processes of the state.[4] Agamben also introduced the Roman law figure of *homo sacer*, someone exiled from social support and protection and whose homicide would bring no legal consequences. The exiled could be forcibly reduced to bare life as they belonged to a class of entities removed from society. Designating a person as *homo sacer* then bestowed the state absolute power over their life—a hair-raising similarity with today's forcibly displaced refugees, shelterless populations, prisoners of war, and, of course, with Indigenous Peoples all over the world.

From the perspective of the Catholic Church, the state represented the only civilized *good life*. This convenient idea made the Church the wealthiest owner of occupied territories and extracted resources from the fourteenth century onward. Through the Doctrine of Christian Discovery of 1493, Pope Alexander VI authorized the Spanish Crown to confiscate Indigenous Lands and Peoples.

Military explorers received a spiritual license to torture, rape, and desacralize our Lands, bodies, and beliefs with such ideas as authorizing the Christian faiths to be lifted and extended throughout the world by subjugating and converting to the faith the "uncivilized countries" and declaring those explorers the lords of these Lands and Peoples, bestowing upon them all kinds of power, authority, and jurisdiction.[5] This license resulted in Indigenous genocide and the near-total extinction of the Native population in Mexico. Ninety percent of Indigenous people is said to have been perished at the hands of the colonizers.[6]

The Spanish crown and the Catholic Church insisted that religious conversion was the only way to raise Indigenous populations to a good life. The Indigenous sense of sacred Nature—and, therefore, of our holy human nature—became a source of threat and terror. And so, Indigenous communities, exiled from our *Tamoanchan,* were dehumanized.

Let us be critical of creating these identity stories because we create what we live by. As we journey further, in the next section, we will consider how we can begin to compost our stories of coloniality and othering for new narratives of belonging and reemergence.

Yes, we carry intergenerational trauma *and also* intergenerational bliss.

Through Bliss We Heal

In the past twenty years, much has been said about historical trauma responses, intergenerational trauma, and how the body retains the memories of disturbing events. While Indigenous tribal cultural differences impact how the wounding manifests across generations and within an individual's lifespan, there is no question of the impact of violence on our bodies.

Our bodies carry the consequences of these horrors, bolting like feral foals at the first blast. Trauma wrecks our interactions, shatters our sleep, and flares like a bonfire with everyday microaggressive interactions of colonial extraction and abuse.

The shards tear into our flesh, over our lifespan and across generations, emanating from massive tribal trauma consequences of cultural genocide due to Land dispossession and loss of language to assimilation.

Such disruptions appear as constellations of events that intrude on our waking and sleep consciousness, generating turmoil and uproar as reactivity: the loss of Lands, the loss of culture, and the loss of bodies.

Being Indigenous means carrying colonial wounds. Our identities today are inextricably linked to the historical colonization, invasion, exploitation, and commodification of our Lands and resources. The result is widespread complex distress of a psychosocial nature.[7]

The past five hundred years of genocide and forced assimilation, along with contemporary and chronic experiences of grief, shame, distrust, anger, and complex traumatic stress, endure in our everyday experience of the world. The broken bones of this cultural and structural system drown our Lands with the blood of our youth. The heartbreaking discoveries of human remains on the grounds of boarding schools in North America bring to the surface the magnitude of grief and bereavement of our population.

To this day, fundamental human rights such as equity, dignity, freedom, and respect are more difficult for Indigenous populations to access due to the legacies of colonialism. Our sacred Landscapes continue to be exploited for economic and political interests, unleashing disease and destruction. And we remain the object of human rights and environmental violations, such as being persecuted, marginalized, dispossessed of Lands, and murdered for defending them.[8]

Indigenous health also continues to be significantly undermined, keeping us at the lowest rates of well-being globally and with an almost indiscernible chance of flourishing.[9] Research has found a correlation between rumination on historical injury and a decrease in well-being for people who culturally identify as having Indigenous heritage. That lack of well-being manifests in not getting married, substance abuse, depression, and anxiety disorders.[10] Fathoming the extreme forms of violence committed against our Peoples for generations leaves indelible scars.

There is no place where Indigenous life expectancy is the same as our non-Indigenous counterparts. In the United States, people from Indigenous Nations live on average six years less than White Americans, and in some areas of the world, the difference is as much as twenty years.[11] According to data from the Center for Disease Control (CDC) National Center for Health Statistics (NCHS), Indigenous life expectancy decreased more than four years due to the pandemic—bringing our average life expectancy to 65, the lowest of countries in the Americas, except Haiti.[12] In fact, the COVID-19 pandemic increased the gap of marginalization, historical structural discrimination, and political exclusion globally, pushing more Indigenous communities to live in poverty without access to safety, housing, clean water, sanitation, and food security.[13]

It is no surprise that the same physiological health-undermining characteristics show up in Indigenous Relatives at the global level. Elevated mortality rates are often caused by so-called "lifestyle diseases" that stem from extreme forms of violence to self and others, including alcohol and substance abuse, suicidal ideations, recklessness, low self-esteem, and anger.[14]

Violence against women and girls persists as global cultural practices but are much more prevalent for Indigenous women and girls. The highest number of victims of human trafficking subjected to sexual exploitation, child marriage, and forced labor are girls and women, with an estimated one in three women suffering physical or sexual abuse in their lives.[15] Marital rape is acceptable by law in 37 countries.[16] Furthermore, female genital mutilation is still culturally accepted in more than 30 countries, where more than 1 in 3 girls aged 15 to 19 have suffered this procedure.[17] Globally, at least 200 million girls and women have been subjected to the practice, most of the time before the age of 5.[18]

Indigenous girls and women are much more vulnerable to these extreme forms of violence, as their identity transcends gender to encompass the inequalities of race, ethnicity, marginalization, access to health services, education, geographical location, and right to self-determination.[19] Such violence is also a direct cultural product of colonialism and coloniality, shaped not only by gender discrimination but also by a context of ongoing militarism, racism, and social and political exclusion.[20]

Over four in five Indigenous women (84.3 percent) have experienced violence in their lifetime in the United States; three out of five have experienced psychological aggression (66.4 percent), and half have been victims of sexual violence (56.1 percent), physical violence (55.5 percent), and stalking (48.8 percent).[21] The murder rate in the United States is ten times higher for Indigenous women, and murder is the third leading cause of death.[22] Furthermore, we are significantly more likely to be raped in our lifetimes.[23] In 2021, these figures prompted the United States government to proclaim May 5th to be Missing and Murdered Indigenous Persons Awareness Day.[24] And yet, Indigenous women are finding ways to reclaim their identity and culture, challenging the deep-seated grief and catastrophic consequences of generations of loss.

In 2022, the women of the Lisu Peoples of China established an entrepreneurial development fund in their Liguang village, providing women with agricultural cultivation, breeding, and processing assistance. Community-protected areas are vital in the relationship between humans and Mother Earth. The Lisu use their traditional knowledge to address community needs while safeguarding natural resources. Capacity trainings enabled Lisu women to determine their priorities and roles as environmental protectors. Now, the women enforce regulations for community-protected areas, and women represent each village.

In another example, women's associations in the forest village of Sechong Lok have become authorities in protecting water-source forests from logging within. They also demand free, prior, and informed consent from the entire village for cutting down trees in their forests. The community reserve has promoted local biodiversity conservation, and more importantly, they have developed public consensus for cooperative maintenance of their natural resource system.[25]

Relating to accounts of individual and collective trauma is extremely complicated. Reckoning with our history moves us from consideration of self to family, community, purpose, and impact on our surroundings. It requires us to reconsider the scope of our presence and impact on the exquisite sensitivity of others. It makes us compassionate to the pain of others and how they hurt from being othered.

Most times, however, trauma has been hidden so far in our memories that we have become numb to it, hidden it, and forgotten about it. It makes it challenging to accept the trauma even exists. In numbness, we intuit something is off. But there is no way to work through the pain when there is no clue what it is. The body tells a story of disease, but the narrative is gone.

Those who know us close can attest to the lava waves under our skin that no tears can mellow. Shattered, we are fractured. Left behind, we are unable to bear our blood. One day we give up. We let the wound open and the blood dry, forgetting we wear deep stains. We become comfortably numb and dissociated. We breathe silently so no one can find us.

We crack and we come to know vulnerability. We see ourselves in others and in them we learn our strength: a shared community. Who we are and how we survive depends on nurturing the other.

The healing principles and actions of the group and personal recovery are the hoop between history, violence, embodied experience, and narratives.

Strength is measured only by collective possibilities of growth and health, weaving all members into our traditions.

We are only as strong as our stories. So we keep telling them . . . reminding us of the resiliency of our Peoples. We may lose everything, but we still have our stories.

Most often individuals do not engage in self-inquiry. Blindfolded, we do not comprehend the psychic and cultural forces that influence our emotions and behaviors. We react to events in whatever environment we are in without examining how the individual is part of a family—part of a culture and its cultural story.

Before engaging in contemplative therapeutic work, we tend to speak of an idealized family story. In the process of digging in, the realities of the human story come to the surface—a story that is made of mess and bliss.

What I have come to understand is that we are our families' stories. We are what our culture has endured. All of those different circles inform who we all are.

Ignoring the origins of our story is perhaps a defense mechanism against what was a really disturbed and yet very human story. A lack of compassion is the result of ignoring our roots, which results in more othering and more trauma.

We must remember we may lose everything, but we still have our stories. The first part of knowing ourselves is finding those stories. The place of blindness and numbness is invariably the beginning of our journey of spiritual becoming. On the path of spiritual becoming, we develop a kind heart. We attain joy through compassion and the collective recognition of our shared fallible humanity.

Yes, the way to bliss is through our mess. And so, we find the courage to dig in it to begin disentangling ourselves and set us free.

PRACTICE

Reverencing Home

Previous practices have exercised the abilities of examination and conversation, prompting us to establish a way of conversing with the Lands, the Peoples, and our perception. Ideally, these are now new friends in the making. The contemplative ability of attention has become a light, making the colored tones of our relationships evident. Through your own experience and analyses, you have proved that contemplation is the art of truth and flourishing the path of connection. Now, I encourage you to add one more step: Reverence as the source of action.

Consider the following precepts:

Reverence is the source of care toward the Homes, the Lands, and the Peoples—Our Ancestors of blood-and-earth lines.

Reverence honors the dignity and presence of others' existence, wisdom, and culture.

Reverence approaches others with humility.

Reverence is the source of moral righteousness and stresses belonging as inherent to life.

Reverence reckons with harm perpetrated.

Reverence repairs atrocities we have benefited from, even unknowingly.

Reverence is the source of accountability to beneficial relationships.

Reverence ensures that everyone belongs and has a home to return to.

Reflecting on these tenets shows that community identities benefit from fairness. At witnessing injury, we demonstrate disgust and seek to alleviate the harm it causes. The dignity that reverence incites translates into protecting the home of our lineages of blood and earth.

But what does this mean? Where is home? Is it a structure, a location, an emotion, a sense of belonging or personhood? How do we know we are at home? How do we find it? How do we protect it?

These are some legitimate questions that we converse with in the following practice, which targets intentional and compassionate connections through reverence for home.

As with other practices, this one is twofold. The first part is a reflective exploration into the question of home that requests you to exercise your contemplative abilities of truth, connection, and the new step of reverence. The second part is an inner dialogue with three interlocutors: home, Lands, and Peoples.

Let yourself be free to explore how the practice moves and transforms you. Do not expect one specific result.

If you haven't done so, turn off your devices or leave them in a different place.

Find a place where you feel comfortable.

Make your chosen place easy to access. Ideally, your practice should be accessible at any time and place in your daily life.

Wherever you are, observe how your surroundings manifest.

Let your body rest in a way that helps you stay relaxed but attentive.

Let your eyes open with a soft gaze, taking a panoramic view.

The path should be gradual, gentle, and soothing yet encourage us to move little by little beyond our comfort zone.

Pause

Settling in the body with our eyes closed,
we go after the texture of our breath.
We follow the light of attention,
illuminating body and breath.

We become the home of attention, body, and breath.

Notice the moment of awareness:

Being Home.

Rest there.

Stay suspended with each moment of bare truth.
Notice how connections flourish from truth.
Host these new friends—your surroundings.

As you let go, notice the porosity of home,
giving and taking—coming and going—you are no more.
You have become home.
Home: hosting, being, and becoming with your surroundings.

What say the surroundings about our Ancestors
our parents and grandparents—before and parallel to them
of blood and bone—of earth and ore?

What were their joys and woes
now unknown, deep down our cores?

Where, who, and what was home to our Siblings
now displaced and lost in mind and bone?

In genocide, enslavement, exploitation . . .
Where is home?

In loss, where is home?
In grief, who is home?
In love, how is home?

Return the breath home.
Notice its response.

Ancestors of Earth and Skies host our breath,
their heart is our home.

Truth, connection, and reverence are home.
Awareness and gratitude are home.
Their stories are our stories and our home.
Our gentle breath is our home:
a shared home:
a home of belonging:
a home of love
is our home.

In the Quest for Insight

As a reminder, the quest for insight exercises aid in integrating your two-fold practice into insights that orient your daily life. The questions guide you to reflect on your perception of truth, relationships, and reverence for the world.

Let these cues animate your experience.

Feel each of them as they rise in the body, heart, mind, memory, imagination, and belonging.

Let them simmer.

Let what connects you to the world emerge.

Invite a conversation with those with whom you share your life and home.

This practice took the path of contemplation as truth, flourishing as connection, and reverence as action. It encourages reflection, conversation, and porous inner-and-outer exploration.

The first explorative part of the practice compels you to reckon with past harmful experiences to our homes, Lands, and Peoples. Becoming accountable for harm against others from which we have benefited, even unknowingly, takes tremendous courage. Nothing less than audacity is needed to repair relationships by dignifying those injured. Dare the bravery.

How would you respond now to the initial questions:

- How does each passing moment as home shape your perception?

- What is home?

- Where is home? Is it a structure, a location, an emotion, a sense of belonging, a sense of personhood?

- How do we identify being at home?

- How do we find home?

- How do we protect our home?

PART 3

Collecting
Well-Being

INDIGENOUS TEACHINGS SPEAK of transcendence as realizing the subtle nuance of relationships. Our contemplative traditions have been tested and refined for their environmental, communal, and individual benefits for millennia. Our traditional knowledges are grounded in principles of embodiment and action-oriented practices that aim for collective well-being. I call these principles: *Kin Relationality*, conceiving all of existence as kin, and *Ecological Belonging*, the understanding that we are each part of a cooperative system and life cycles. Humans flourish as we awaken to our responsibility as caretakers of the ecosystem. Our life path is the opportunity to sublimate a collective mind made of relations—a new, radical way of being based on kin relationality and ecological belonging. Thus, through connection, we start our journey through the Indigenous foundations for collective well-being.

Flourishing Kin is at the heart of cultivating an insightful, collective, practice-based, flexible identity. As such, storytelling, cultural tradition, and other forms of enhanced contemplative practice, like ritual, music, movement, and art, support our journey through this section. The following principles are the seeds we will be watering to let our sense of kin flourish in the following chapters:

Kin Relationality is our ability to perceive all living beings as Relatives—a perspective shared by Indigenous Peoples worldwide.

Body Seed explores the body as a vessel of experience and as an expansion of the roots that connect us to a sense of place and our shared Lands around the globe.

Senshine, a playful coming together of senses and sunshine, looks at how we use our senses to brighten our life experience. It nurtures the observation of direct experience as a source of traditional wisdom.

Heartfelt Wisdom focuses on the power of emotions to orient our skillful action for planetary flourishing. Here, storytelling compels positive, other-focused transcendent emotions such as reverence, gratitude, compassion, kindness, awe, love, and sacredness.

Ecological Belonging renews our awareness of being part of the extensive Earth system, eliciting a commitment to care for it and raising nature-based contemplation and narratives of belonging.

Reparations Through Right Relationships offers engaged ethical principles suggesting pathways for reparation, restoration, and the return of benefits to Mother Earth and Indigenous Peoples.

Reemerging is the next cycle of the spiral path of collective well-being, returning to the observation, embodiment, narrative, and reflection of shared experience.

7

Kin Relationality

ORIGIN STORIES OR cosmogonies tell us of the early stages of the Universe when nothing was yet formed, labeled, nor given meaning. All laid contained in a *prima materia*—a primordial sort of cosmic ocean of potentiality. All of life's creation rested latent, dormant, in repose. Quiet.

Western science tells us of another—not too dissimilar—cosmogony. In this model, the Universe's early stages are scorching temperatures burning all of existence in its primordial element of fire. This high-density force of creativity elicited a big bang from which the universe continues to expand to the present day.

These two symbolic models reveal something undeniable: before anything rises, it is contained in its entirety of chaos, complexity, and plurality. This potentiality explodes into expansive possibilities that gradually pursue an order of resonance—a cosmos. Thus, narratives arise with cosmogonic meaning. *Kosmos*: order. *Gonos*: seed. The seed of the Universe contains all potential, then sprouts in narratives of interpretative meaning.

Consider the following first words of the Nahua and Maya cosmogonies:

In oc yohuaya
in ayamo tona
in ayamo tlathui . . .

When it was all darkness
when there was no sun
when there was yet no dawn

—*Leyenda de los Soles (Nahua)*

Kalal spisil chijan tinal
J'ojcholal ma chal nax
Ta ij q'uinal . . .

When everything was silent
empty of meaning
in stillness, in darkness

—*Popol Vuh (Maya)*

These seeds are the raw material and fertilizing agent of our presence
on this planet. Indigenous origin stories are multidimensional—from
the *prima materia* in a state of disarray to the creation of the world.
They are cosmic, ecological, cultural, and personal, giving way to the
order of planetary responsibility from the cosmos, the planet, the community, and humanity. They give us an origin point that orients us in
the immensity of life. They offer a beginning to the beginningless times,
a grounding to the ever-expansive space, and a significance to the mer-
ciless passing of impermanence.

The Nahua cosmogonies speak of humans as coming from ashes and
blood—the ashes of the bones of previous eras and the blood of divine
beings. The Hopi speak of being made of earth and saliva. The Maya tell
us of living beings made of the sacred corn and Spirit, coming together
from earth and lightning. At its core, each narrative is a welcoming into
the world. They reveal the heart of the holy, weaving waves of awe.

These stories deal with the creation, development, and reemergence of
the world from celestial bodies to earthlings. They show what constitutes
"right" livelihood: sustainable and honorable ways to be participants and
creators responsible for this very world. They lay out the social context
of a culture, its vision of the world, the conception of its history, its time
orientation, its religious beliefs and practices, and its moral values.

Following this line of thinking, I am raising a new origin story for
the science of flourishing, the current happiness and contemplative paradigm, and the ethics of belonging. I do so by starting not with how the

individual develops and refines the self nor how different practices bring personal benefits. Quite the opposite, I start with the formation of the world itself, containing all potentiality in its chaos and disarray. I will tell the story of how it progressively finds its order and meaning in the cosmos, the planet, the community, and the individual.

I will show how in an ecosystem of flourishing kin, new cosmologies grow from seeds of reverence, respect, and responsibility. How these concerted actions manifest inner truths about life, being, and belonging in deep gratitude to all our relations. How we flourish to the extent that we enact our exceptional capacity for creation and participation in the nourishing, relational, empowering, and transformative force of Mother Earth.

From the Chaos of the Acorn to the Cosmos of the Grove

All living beings are assumed to be subject to the same natural patterns of chaos and order: creation, decay, and regeneration. The sense of belonging engendered by understanding these cycles helps to integrate personal experience within the ecosystem. The result is an identity rooted in belonging and relationality.

Here, I highlight how Indigenous contemplative wisdom informs all of our relationships through story, shared ritual, and ceremony as inquiry forms, bringing a relational aspect into the physical, emotional, mental, and spiritual liminal spaces. As we've seen, Indigenous traditions in the West have prioritized a space for spiritual connection and reverence, but they have lost much of their sense of the sacred.

Since relationships are central to Indigenous cosmovisions, self and world perception is relational in nature. This kindred method exposes a receptive network of connections infused with reverence, wonder, accountability, and a feeling of sacred relationships. The obligation then spreads to our environmental community. Indigenous identities around the world are firmly anchored in a duty to protect interdependent ecosystems and life cycles, despite their inherent pluralities.

My Ancestors infused my experiences with a relational identity that views the ecosystem as kin. In early childhood, I too listened to the rivers' songs, sensed the jaguar leave its spotted pace upon my veins, and befriended greensome birds. I have found a very similar ethos guiding Indigenous Nations around the globe.

Indigenous perspectives around the world are strikingly similar in their belief that all creation is related. This form of relating embraces the qualities of mutuality, organization, belonging, purpose, and meaning inherent in each phenomenon. All living beings have a part and a purpose in the vast web of relationships. The keen observation of relationships as they interrelate and influence this extensive web is the foundation of our Kin Relationality.

Kin relationality necessitates that we recognize our affiliations and our interdependence on each other and our natural environment. A spiritual binding brings together all human, more-than-human, and environmental relationships through utmost respect for Mother Earth. It orients our actions toward growing communal benefit.

Indigenous traditions cultivate awareness and orientation of kin relationality vis-á-vis all beings and phenomena, engendering gratitude, responsibility, awe, and reverence toward the collective of Mother Earth. The keen observation of phenomena—their origins, conditions, and interrelationships—is the subject and object of contemplative living. Through fierce examination and discernment, trust, and compassion, Indigenous cosmovisions make sense of being through balance, surrendering, community, and establishing collaboration and gratitude toward flourishing kin.

As the world has become more individualistic, our ways of relating have shifted. We are more focused on our differences and adversarial traits. We have turned to othering and separateness, which has given rise to epidemics of loneliness and self-harm. Kin relationality is an antidote to these trends. Through kin relationality, we experiment and evaluate relational processes rather than being subject to established conventions based on the self. This relational system encourages the physical, emotional, cognitive, and spiritual qualities that make Indigenous systems profoundly diverse and ecological. Ultimately, kin relationality is a path to sustainable collective well-being.

Indigenous traditions with deep cultural roots in contemplative wisdom hold critical and timely solutions to our most pressing social and environmental injustices. For millennia, Indigenous Peoples all over the world—in their distinct uniqueness, multiplicity, and plurality—have developed keen perceptions of the consciousness of Mother Earth. Time and again, the teachings of embodied knowledge appear in various forms of Indigenous wisdom. These diverse traditional ways point to a relational capacity based on collaboration, compassion, and reverence for Life.

The forestlands open the hidden waters to the skies. They direct our journey of belonging and becoming in a dream of collective effervescence, a ceremony, a shared experience of Spirit-making. We enact the story of belonging to our Earth by becoming beings of reverence, kindness, and compassion. We turn to ashes to return in the breath of Life. We come back transformed, reunited, and reemerged. What can transform the basic nature of the acorn into the spiritual awareness of the grove? It is its chrysopoeia, its metamorphosis, its evolution from self-interest to collective flourishing.

Kin Relationality and Collective Flourishing

A kin relational practice may entail visualizing becoming a resting seed nourished by the web of relationships in the generous, openhearted, embracing home that is the fertile soil of Mother Earth. Such a practice cultivates a sense of safety by simulating a feeling of being held by a primordial Earth Mother.

At its core, Indigenous contemplation entails becoming acquainted with the relationships among all beings as part of the larger, responsive system of Mother Earth. Contemplative practices like the ones you have experienced through *Flourishing Kin* strengthen the communal bond of kin relationality, eliciting feelings of familiarity and safety. This familiarity allows us to trust we can respond creatively and constructively to our web of kin relationships. It allows for easeful observation of our connections.

Trusting the web of relationships does not mean the absence of threats. Instead, it orients us to a response that promotes flow and encourages inner and outer balance. This ability to interpret and integrate the internal sensory input of experiential processes is known as interoception.[1] It enables awareness, body regulation, intention, motivation, and reward assessment. It drives the spiral path between feelings and behaviors.

A new Western science of belonging, connectivity, and kindness aligns with these insights of Indigenous kin relationality practices. Regions of the brain, like the periaqueductal gray, the vagus nerve, and oxytocin networks, support openness to others, kindness, and the foundations of kin relationality.[2] When I practice kin relationality, I feel these ancient physiological systems as a warmth in my chest, a sense of calm and openness, and even the occasional tearing in my eyes.

Our survival, and that of our hyper-dependent offspring, depend on connection, collaboration, and belonging within webs of relationships. Mammals depend on caregivers for long periods to develop the adaptive functions crucial for health and survival. In humans, who have the longest offspring dependency of all primates, mother-infant and close kin interactions are collaborative strategies for reducing the rate of mortality and favoring security across the life span.[3] Findings on social psychology confirm that a sense of safety is elicited by such strong social bonds and that cultivating a sense of kin relationality, enabled by basic forms of communication, like eye contact and touch, brings about that feeling of being held. Furthermore, the neuroscience of emotion shows that the same neural regions that process safety and a sense of protection inhibit physiological threat responses.[4]

Along these lines, immersion in Mother Earth—natural environments are vital places to cultivate kin relationality—has proved to be one of the most robust predictors of enhanced physical health, subjective well-being, and prosocial, community-enhancing behavior.[5] More specifically, research suggests that interrelating with the natural environment increases parasympathetic activity, promotes stress relief, and enhances immune system function.[6]

In other words, when humans feel a sense of safety and kinship with Mother Earth, we flourish. Our nervous systems increase the parasympathetic activity that induces stress relief.[7] Likewise, the immune system shows higher levels of antibodies and lower adrenaline in the blood.[8] Psychological health significantly improves due to decreased hostility and depression.[9] In fact, cultivating such a sense of Mother Earth belonging—or kin relationality—has been found to increase life expectancy by ten years.[10]

These studies reveal the underlying physiology of what you might experience when engaging in practices that cultivate kin relationality. Being held within the larger Mother Earth system, being in the presence of something vast and larger than ourselves, brings us a sense of awe that diminishes the self-centered identity and allows for the possibility of deepening our relations with others and finding our place within community.[11] It allows for collective flourishing.

Collective flourishing stems from the sense of relationality at the core of belonging. Kin relationality raises awareness of our responsibility for others and the impact of our behavior on others. Synergistically, these experiences broaden our thought patterns and make us aware of the physical, social, and psychological resources that can empower us.

Indigenous collective practices support multiple dimensions of flourishing that extend to more-than-humans and planetary systems. Kin relationality enhances environmental stewardship. By advancing the study of kin relationality through Indigenous and Western sciences, I hope to broaden and strengthen our understanding of how contemplation can elicit planetary flourishing and health and how the sciences of contemplation, flourishing, and happiness can enable a world of collective participation and empowerment.

Kin Relationality

Just like other practices we have engaged with throughout the book, the first part of this practice encourages you to delve into present exploration and observation. In the second part, you will explore the intuitive aspects of an interactive conversation with your relationships by following your perception without labeling. Don't anticipate a single outcome. Give yourself permission to investigate how the practice affects and changes you.

The kin relationality practice below aims at bringing you greater emotional flourishing, happiness, and well-being. And in keeping with Indigenous approaches, we will orient these benefits of kin relationality to planetary flourishing.

This practice of kin relationality was orally transmitted through the words and rhythms of my lineage and the voices of my childhood's forests, winds, and rivers.

A kin relationality practice stimulates connection and awareness of relationship systems by actively engaging with Mother Earth and our more-than-human Relatives. Our belonging in Nature is one of our most profound forms of relationality, shaped over millennia of social evolution. Studies show that cultivating kin relationality brings us a greater sense of connection, prosocial physiological activation, and a sense of reverence, responsibility, kindness, and awe. Through kin relationality, we awaken to the sacredness of Mother Earth.

Find a comfortable, safe place—preferably outdoors, should you have the privilege of greenery. Turn off your devices or put them somewhere else if you haven't already.

Locate a spot where you are at ease.

Make the location you've chosen accessible. Ideally, you should be able to access your practice anywhere at any time during your daily routine.

No matter where you are, pay attention to how your environment appears.

Allow your body to repose in a way that keeps you alert and at ease.

Gently open your eyes and take in the expansive view.

The journey should be calm, easy, and gradual while gradually pushing you to step outside your comfort zone.

Let's begin by pausing.

We start by bringing our attention to Mother Earth.
She is our container and vessel of nourishment.
She is our place for action and becoming.

Welcome Her as She welcomes you: open and bare.
If you're wearing shoes or socks or sandals, take them off.
Let the soles of your feet feel the texture of the ground.
Sense the Lands, feel the Lands, get to know them.

Let your gaze expand from behind your eyelids into the horizon.
So your ear opens to the gentle hum around you.
Then your taste, your skin, your heart
meet the world around you.

Sense the sudden and the subtle change of light.
Enjoy the playfulness of the games of the shadow, the color, and the form.

All our Relatives become apparent.
Some are curious. Some go on with their chores.

Mother Earth opens to welcome you.
She holds you in Her container of safety.
Pay attention to how Mother Earth feels under your feet.
How grounded and reliable She feels.
She is.
Always there for you.
Mother Earth will catch you when you fall.

Open to Her.
Tend to Her.
Connected.
Grounded.
Rooting into Her, you enter Mother Earth.

Your roots from the tip of your toes dive in,
digging deep into the soil.
Twisting, turning, and discovering.

Continue until you find a chamber
in the vast and fertile
beautiful pitch-blackness of Mother Earth.

You are a seed resting in this chamber
Opening to all potentiality.

A well, swelling of possibilities, flows within, through,
and all around you.
Myriad beings, material and subtle, around you hold and nourish you.

You are safe.
You are held.
You are allowed to be content.
You are protected.
You belong.

The world is in this seed.
It opens through you to discover.

As you open, sense your surroundings.
The beautiful, caring, nourishing Mother Earth is bringing medicine.
It is the healing, nourishing sap of love.
It is flowing into your seed
of wellness.

It flows through your roots
twisting, turning, and discovering . . .

Upward goes to the tip of your toes into the soles of your feet,
your thighs, the base of the spine,
and the center of your chest into your heart.
The medicine expands to your whole chest
allowing for a full, deep breath of o p e n n e s s

Swell in that breath.
Allow that sap of love to continue upward into the crown of your head.
It reaches out into the Skies, embracing the whole world around you.

Let that love pour like rain gently on the whole world around you.

Your gaze meets the swelling all around you.
Opening to you too.

Outward, reaching all our Relatives,
inward, flows the love back to you,
and again into the well of Mother Earth.

Your gaze is now porous and goes through you into all beings.
All these Relatives turn at you, smiling.
You smile back.
We share our wellness, our presence, our light and our shadow.
The sap of wellness and belonging comes together with our world.

Together, right here.

Right now.

In the Quest for Insight

Remind yourself that this search for understanding will lead you through a few cues to deepen this contemplation and reveal more about how your view of the world interacts with you.

Allow yourself to be animated by these cues. As they arise in the body, heart, mind, memory, imagination, and sense of belonging, feel each one of them.

Give them time to simmer.

Allow what binds you to the world to come to light.

Seeking understanding should not end with introspection; instead, start a dialogue with the people you live with.

- What places visited your practice? How did they arise in images, sensations, emotions?

- Who came to visit? How did they connect? What senses did they reach?

- How do you relate to these beings and phenomena?

Take a few moments.

Hold the experience.

Embrace it.

Thank it.

Now, let it go . . .

Write some notes in your cherished contemplative journal-chest.

To listen to this practice, follow the link yuriacelidwen.com
or the QR code on the table of contents.

8

Body Seed

THE ENVIRONMENT IS made of phenomena, and the body itself is phenomena manifesting as experience, raw and intricate, as complex materials varying in subtlety. The properties of the body arise when all processes flow in unison—not atomic or isolated but collectively emergent.

Think of the body as a seed of arising influences stemming from interactions. The dynamic progression of combinations creates functioning systems that stimulate life. All bodies are made of these ongoing combinations that weave themselves into the environment. The body uses these materials to generate knowledge of itself and its environment while at the same time interacting to procure its nourishment from the very oxygen we breathe.

Consider that a cell cannot offer nutrition without awareness of and dependence on other collective processes that form organs and systems of organs. That is to say, without a body seed, there is no forest grove, no cognizance of Mother Earth. The two are interrelated in a system of constantly arising phenomena.

Indigenous cosmologies understand this interrelationality as much more than just a collection of biological processes. We understand the body as a seed, a home to experience and potentiality, a container in and of communities. We observe the body as interdependent on all other bodies and perceive them as nourishing planetary health. We recognize them as spiritual processes honoring the impulse of continuity.

Concepts of the Body—Mother Earth

The pre-Inca Andean Kallawaya (or *Qollahuaya*) Peoples belong to the Mollo Tiwanaku culture of the highland Andean area of western Bolivia. Initially a nomadic group, they eventually settled in Peru and migrated as far south as Argentina. Known as the *Qolla Kapachayuh,* or "Lords of the Medicine Bag," their *khapchos* bags contain medicines, formulas, and amulets, similar to the medicine wrap the Maya medicine people carry. The Qolla see the body as a Mother Earth–map model that directly correlates to their Lands, named *ayllu,* or "mountain of three vertical ecological levels with a central axis."

Notably, the Kallawaya perceive their Lands as forming a larger holy body. This mountain body is composed of limbs connected by rivers that flow energy, much like the human body's vascular system. The Lands constitute a relational unit working together, interdependent on their elements for balance, including the human community. The mountain body is just like an anatomical body unit. As with the Nahua entities, the principal body fluids that contain prime vital energy, such as blood and fat, come together at the heart and flow through the limbs of the body, carrying vitality.[1]

A not-too-dissimilar example is from the high, snowcapped mountains of the Altai Peoples, whose love of their Lands is expressed in their epic story of the wise flying horse that never steps on the grass to avoid disheveling Mother Earth's beautiful hair. The word *Altai* means "home, country, and the whole of their Lands," making clear their reverence for the body of Mother Earth.

Indigenous sciences consider how the body seed retains memories—intergenerational and self-experienced—in the body's constitution. Consequently, we investigate how experiences elicit the fluid color of appraisal. Gradually, we work on awareness of arousals in the body from environment, affect, sensation, adaptation, and response. Then we return to the environment to modulate our responses while embracing them fully. And it becomes clear: the body, as a seed of knowledge, is rooted in the bountiful soil of Mother Earth's kin relationality.

Body Seed and Kin Relationality

The body is not an isolated atomic entity. It interacts with its environment in processes that manifest the world inside out, from the acorn to the grove. With kin relationality, we realize how we are part of planetary systems. Once we can comprehend the web of relations through kin relationality, we begin to comprehend the body by experiencing its own phenomena as relationships. We are a body in and of communities. Sensations, emotions, thoughts, and actions make the body a seed in and of communities. Within our body seeds, these systems are not a part of us—they *make* us. We are the sheer fabric through which these myriad experiences flow.

With kin relationality, we began to develop essential skills. Physical competence relates to the examination and dialogue with our physical ease, arousal, or rest. Emotional finesse involves building trust in the community, embracing the diversity of life. Ecological humility expands our experiences of awe at the vastness of Nature. Cognitive prowess entails observing relations through the analysis of universal and contextual input. Character development follows motivation and participation in the benefit of the larger community. It is based on approaching relations through curiosity, service, kindness, and gratitude. Finally, ethical mastery comes in the fruit of care and concern for our environment. These capacities are the connective ties to appreciating others and eliciting a desire and action to alleviate collective distress.

The body seed principle further develops these skills and turns them inward. It investigates the various phenomena involved in bodily processes through the flow approach of Indigenous contemplation. It reveals how the body brings us to the direct experience of internal relational processes. It teaches us that our trust in Mother Earth systems must be as intentional and fierce as our bodily trust in these internal processes.

With this principle, physical skill development involves refining the observation of functions arising in the body—of reflecting, regulating, and adapting their flow for the generation of balance. The emotional abilities of trust are now about accepting the changes in states and perceptions with gentleness.

Our cognitive skills now analyze the body's response to the environment and its impact. More importantly, it intentionally discerns environmental well-being. Character development comes from a curiosity about these relations and how they are regulated through self-kindness and gratitude for the body as a relational universe. The ethical aspect arises from comprehending how the actions and care directed to our bodies are the same as those Mother Earth requires.

From visualizing the outer web of environmental relating, we turn to investigate the inner web of relations. We attune the body to the direct experience of kin relationality. As a result, the body regains balance and flow. It is in itself rooting connectedness. In this way, we allow the weaving of new memories that nourish the direct experience of the relational self in a responsive world.

We water the body as the seed of kindness, reverence, and respect. We make meaning through experience.

Observing kin relationality in the Lands and culture dictates the body seed's responses. We follow the dynamics of the body and the environment and how they constitute each other. We observe these relationship undercurrents that manifest in emotion, arousal, adaptation, response, and reemergence of experience in the body.

As we tend to the elemental body seed, we become familiar with the components of experience and realize, once again, that we are all a web of interacting phenomena. As a seed, the body depends on the environment for adequate nourishment to survive and flourish. The body is a vessel of experience germinating an emergent shoot. This shoot is awareness. Such awareness is the ground for halting threat reactivity, for opening to our common humanity and shared need for mutual care and kindness.

Two main interconnected paths are central to this pursuit of awareness. The first is the environmental dynamics of kin relationality, and the second is the body seed's interior phenomenology. Using these foundations, we aim to observe internal phenomena through direct experience in order to recognize how social and cultural preconceptions modify our responses. From there, we aspire to direct these responses intentionally toward kindness, compassion, reverence, awe, love, and sacredness.

Direct experience is an effortless, full presence that does not label or appraise phenomena through sociocultural conditioning. Direct experience means interacting with phenomena precisely *as they are*. Spontaneous cases of direct experience happen more often than we imagine. Any moment of absorption that claims us is a taste of direct experience. It opens the tongues of each of our pores and the true flavor of the phenomena bursts in its presence.

Most likely, you have been immersed in such moments more often than your yearning can remember.

When time dissolves its grip, we are here.
Time haste and constrained turn docile, tamed, and pliable.
Space turns porous and permeable.
Possibility recedes, flexes, and opens.
There is no more chasing or evading or absconding.
We are again in the blissful womb of presence.
Because nothing is, everything is possible.

These moments are similar to flow—the state of hyperfocus toward a specific goal that inspires us to engage in an exciting activity, eliciting challenge, delight, and enjoyment.[2] However, while flow implies an *action*, direct experience is a *state of being*.

Sidenote: Direct experience is a familiar competence of traditional healers, who tend to enter into states of rapture from an early age without particular training to elicit them. In some traditions, these experiences are one of many indications of a person's suitability for the responsibility of becoming a community healer. When a child presents these aptitudes, they may enter into an apprenticeship with a medicine Elder to develop the skills that prompt and harness these experiences so they can be employed in service to the community's health. However, direct experience and its development as a skill of service are the outskirts of Indigenous contemplative practice.

The Body as Seed of Compassion

How we experience emotions is influenced by how we assess our interactions and how successfully these interactions meet our needs. This approach suggests that finesse in appraising emotions will result in a better sense of subjective experience.[3]

The Indigenous contemplative approach gives us a feasible path to refine our emotional appraisal skills. In fact, a crucial goal of Indigenous contemplative practice—and many other contemplative traditions—is learning how to respond intentionally to our subjective experience.

Let's consider the distinct emotions that arise from environmental interactions and their physiological manifestations (that is, our body responses) using the four skills for observing the body: (1) emotional appraisal, (2) interoception, (3) cognition and metacognition, and (4) systems influence. I will explain each of these skills using the example below.

Let's say anger arises from witnessing injustice between groups with historic power differentials (emotional appraisal). That anger elicits an increase in heart rate, blood pressure, and respiration, prompting the adrenal glands to produce stress hormones and to force blood to the muscles to prepare for action. The body temperature rises, resulting in perspiration (interoception). Reduced heart-rate variability stimulates the sympathetic nervous system to assess the best path of action for defense or confrontation (cognition). A substantial body response prompts self-regulation by lengthening the breath. As the body calms down, one can initiate negotiations (metacognition). Finally, a regulated response encourages a conversation based on respect and gentleness, which lowers the stress response of the groups in question attempting a bridging dialogue of possible agreements benefiting both (systems influence).

Now, think of compassion and how this emotion arises from perceiving the suffering of self or others. The body response involves the interoception of an increased heartbeat in preparation for the physical exertion that accompanies our actions to alleviate others' distress. The recognition of gratitude increases the activity of the vagus nerve, generating an outburst of parasympathetic nervous system activity associated with feelings of contentment and safety.[4] All these phenomena can be observed and followed in the body, and more importantly, they serve as the grounds for the intentional cultivation of positive relationships.[5]

I imagine very similar body responses occur when we practice kin relationality. Indigenous contemplation elicits an awareness of the interdependence of systems, of kinship and mutuality. In turn, an appreciation of kin elicits a kindred compassion in which the wish to alleviate others' afflictions is not from a removed standpoint—the current Western view—but rather the enactment of care because care is mutually beneficial.[6] This Indigenous perspective of a body, in which appraisals of environmental dynamics influence responses, reduces the experience of overwhelming and hostile phenomena.

Indigenous cosmovisions of Mesoamerica and the Andean region (Maya, Mixtec, Misak, Miskito, Mapuche, Quechua, Ashaninka, to name a few), emphasize a cosmic relational influence for attaining balance. These Indigenous cosmovisions consider the environmental impact on the body and how that influence may promote or disturb homeostasis.

The Mesoamerican Nahua, Maya, Mixtec, and Zapotec Peoples appraise qualities of experience by categories of temperature directly related to the life force of the Sun (*kin* in Maya). A medicine person looks into how these containers of Sun influence the body and how much heat is in any interaction. Warmth, which is considered to be present in all bodies, influences all phenomena, from fungi, animals, and plants to rocks, gusts of wind, storms, and even environmental containers like caves or forest groves. Thus, warmth or coolness is the basis of this traditional medicine. These remedies are known as *kinam xiuoob*, herbs of the Sun, or herbs of health and virtue.

An Indigenous-Western scientific method can help us achieve a more diversified and possibly granular following of subjective experience that takes the environment into account. The benefits reaped from such a practice are beneficial not only for the individual or even for the human species but also for the more extensive system of Mother Earth—from the cultivation of collective active emotional virtues such as kindness, compassion, gratitude, awe, and a sense of reverence, love, and sacredness.

The Body Seed and Collective Flourishing

Indigenous cosmovisions guide our ways of being in a complex system of traditional knowledge based on unique languages, practices, needs, and customs transmitted orally through generations. Observation of environments led to the formation of cultures that generated further awareness of the body. For example, observing landscapes helped us to understand natural cycles with the environment and within our bodies as a means to cultural and personal equilibrium. This way of being gave rise to contemplative living.

We can extend this way of being to our understanding that healing environmental damage is akin to attaining spiritual purification and balance. This Earth-based endemic way of living agrees that human health originates from a healthy environment and returns us to the central insight that *there is no human flourishing without Mother Earth flourishing first.*

Bodies and Lands are determinants of health beyond the individual and community levels; they are determinants of the sustainable collective well-being and flourishing of Mother Earth. Our bodies intertwined with the Lands reclaim our place, our territories, and our rights over the sovereignty of resources and food systems.

Think of the body as the seed of the interconnected phenomena that result from being, actions, social transformation, and identity narratives. As contextual worldviews are weaved within Lands and oriented toward ways of being, the body becomes the expression of our spirituality, medicine systems, institutions, governance, ecological management, artistic expressions, and interactions. The body is the ground where we compost defeating narratives and sow seeds against the cataclysm of heartbreak and genocide. It is where we become the catalyst of transformation.

Years of failed interventions have found that Western medicine models of diagnosis and treatment of historical trauma fall short in Indian Country. Perhaps it is that a colossal collective form of *mal del alma,* or "wounded soul," befell the world from the insurmountable greed of colonialist settler advancements. It may very well be that what ails us is cultural-responsive, and so it should be addressed by cultural models of treatment that sing the songs we heard in childhood—those that come from and go back into our Lands, our Ancestors, and the very heart of Mother Earth.

Earlier education designs of American institutions aimed at "killing the Indian and saving the man."[7] In the name of education and social mobility, we were and continue to be separated from our families and culture—trauma that my lineage and I experienced in the flesh. Rejection and loss of social connectedness results in escalated evaluations of threat. It pushes people to further isolate, leading to increased feelings of loneliness, anxiety, depression, and anger.[8] This applies to groups as much as it does to individuals.

As such, liberating the body from these narratives of isolation is critical to our collective flourishing.

We are in quest of flourishing through relationships, reclaiming our cultures, communities, and traditional cultural practices (language, dress, naming) that preserve our identities. Through these roots, we articulate, make sense of, and recover from the wounds we carry from historical oppression.[9]

An Indigenous contemplative lifestyle integrates communal and personal life. Its environmental resolve centers on observing and reverencing cosmic Spirit and recognizing our human part and purpose. Our contemplations are not intended to serve the self; they are a means of service to the planetary community. *Contemplative flourishing is a path of truth and connection.*

Caring for others and caring for self are similar skills.[10] Similarly, sensitivity to others' distress and providing for others' needs both originate from responses of love, kindness, and helpfulness.[11] Furthermore, exposure to outsiders, even for one week, can create the familiarity needed to elicit a helpful response. These conditions show how community environmental assessment is central to our neurophysiological systems.

Indigenous health interventions intentionally introduce actions directed to the community at all levels: community, family, and individual. They reflect our traditions of purposeful and strong relationships for personal and communal well-being and have been proved to prevent the growing impacts of historical trauma.

To solve the social and physical ailments shattering the bodies and hearts of our Peoples caused by historical ravaging, we can apply Indigenous solutions adapted to this time and space. We can bridge Indigenous cultural strengths with Western technical and treatment skills, from the various therapies of clinical psychology to the arts and forms of medicine that start to center in enhancing social relationships and connected communities.

We can start with recognizing kin relationality, setting a safe environment, and empowering the skills conducive to holding, listening, and giving words to our horrors. Giving an ear to our bodies of Mother Earth roots us in a courageous naming and detection of the sources of disease and its influences.

We can look into people's eyes and listen to their stories. We can hold space for the rising memories of events, as painful as they are and in whatever form they want to come and be recalled. This way of being with can only come first from Mother Earth and then from the people themselves.

We can see the body as a part of a social group. We can pay keen attention to how each member contributes to strengthening the structure of relations by nourishing affiliation and collective flourishing along the lifespan. Adults as providers of safety, shelter, and nourishment. Elders as the holders of tradition, who transmit the growth and negotiation of collaborative relationships through the telling of a cultural array of positive stories, rituals, and ceremonies. Children as students of our collective identities and moral codes and the more nuanced ways to sustain our cooperative alliances and supportive reciprocal hierarchies.

We live in a changing world and so we create assemblies to discuss how we will transmit and apply our traditional knowledge of social development and collaboration to aid in collective flourishing. But returning to our ways of being, knowing, and healing may not benefit only Indigenous Peoples. It is a way to bring diverse and rich knowledge to our Earth community at large.

The urgent planetary emergency demands determination and resolve. Grounding our footing on Mother Earth makes our exploration manageable and imperative. Re-membering our bodies—putting them back together—with Mother Earth makes them pathways to personal, community, and planetary healing.

Our bodies become paths to recognizing our strength and collective power. We honor in our bodies our roots and our wisdom for solutions. Through our bodies, we take back the power of Mother Earth to heal life. Our bodies bear the mess and make a dwelling of bliss. We are the cocoon of hope for a heart full of yearning.

PRACTICE

Body Seed

Common mindfulness practices begin by focusing on a single object, usually a body part or process. The most known method has the locus on the breath, while the second most widespread practice is the body scan, which shifts the focus of attention throughout the body. The extensive practices of breath and body scanning have brought tremendous personal benefits to practitioners worldwide; however, their source, Buddhist traditions, aimed to contribute not solely to individual health but had the loftier aspiration of community well-being.

Buddhism as a religion in Asia began as a colonial practice, much like how Christianity was forced onto much of the world. Buddhists place a strong emphasis on compassion for the community; however, they also assume that humans are superior to other living beings because of their extraordinary cognitive abilities. But like syncretic practices of Indigenous and Catholic origin, Bön Buddhism, the fifth branch of Tibetan Buddhism, is still shaped by rituals involving spirits of the Lands influenced by relationships with their environment. These include healing, afterlife, and divination rituals that may entail making animal sacrifices to environmental deities in an effort to bring prosperity to all. For instance, during Losar, the Tibetan new year, Bön practitioners make sheep figurines out of toasted barley flour called *tsampa* and eat a sheep's head in observance of the prosperity of Spirit. Sheep heads are also frequently found in ritual sites frequented by Bön practitioners.

Other forms of body practice exist from the wealth of traditions of the world, from contemplative movement and dance to visualization, chanting, and many others. Here, I invite you to practice an Indigenous approach that concentrates on the body as a system, grounding awareness into the ensemble of phenomena interacting with the environment. I invite you to participate in the creation of collective Spirit awareness.

Holding the body seed draws on resiliency approaches and empowerment for the reemergence of creative experiences. Generally, practicing outdoors brings immediate benefits simply because Mother Earth has a special magic for re-membering our bodies from the dislocated, vulnerable experience of being human. However, if being outdoors is not possible, do not make yourself rigid by demanding a perfect environment. We learn to be wherever we are in whatever way we happen to be. It is a practice in itself to find roots, awe, and home anywhere, starting with our own bodies.

While innumerable gross and subtle phenomena may be overwhelming and distracting—perhaps driving us to hide away—let us practice observing all these streams of experience, staying rooted yet flexible in the struggle. Let us become bamboo, taking the first years of life below the surface just to establish out roots. Then, we shoot upward, knowing Mother Earth holds us and that we are flexible and capable of bending to play with the storming winds.

Permit your body to sit in a way that maintains your alertness and comfort. We slowly see the vast vista around us.

The process should be smooth, easy, and gradual while progressively pushing us to move beyond our comfort zones.

As with other practices, we take the path of thorough examination, memory, and comprehension. The practice is an inquiry on how you sense your body and how you embody relationships and interactions. After you have engaged in dialogue with your shared experience, consider how the presence of each impacts the two of you. Have a conversation with your practice.

Turn off your devices or put them somewhere else if you haven't already. Look for somewhere where you may sit at ease. Take a seat outside and enjoy the scenery if the weather permits. If not, pick a location that lets you take in whatever scenery surrounds you.

Make your selected location easily accessible. Ideally, you should be able to access your practice anywhere at any time during your daily routine.

Pause

Let the winds become your wild child.
Give back the breeze a soft caress.
The winds are part of the stream of occurrences in the vast Skies of awareness.

This is the story of the very essence.
The self-containing and self-creating beginningless essence
that is love.
Everything is in it,
undifferentiated.

In stillness
everything is suspended
In repose
In silence.

Nothing is yet named
Nothing moves
It all is quiet.

Total emptiness
in the vast beautiful pitch blackness
in the waters of the very depths of night.

The Sun of Wind brings the first breath.
He whispers sweet nothings to the waters,
who respond titillating,
making waves
in a cohesive
constant flow.

From the whisper grows the thunder:
fire and the fast-arousing storm
an invisible bliss yearning for touch.

The waters open
forth comes the Mother Earth
expanding
and contracting
embracing
and embraced.

Space and time
day and night
fungi, plant, bird, and beast
rocks, caves, and cliffs.

First human and first breath
sharing life divine.

Things come together
things come apart
approaching
and receding.

We are silent
We make noise

Body
Mind
Heart
and Spirit
unveil the presence
of transcendence and return
a never-ending weaving of the waves of awe . . .

Take a few moments to stay with your experience.
Let it be.
Let go of labels and expectations.
Be with what rises.
Let it be the struggle.
Let it be the bliss.

Re-member until both continue to flow.

In the Quest for Insight

To refresh your memory, the quest for insight leads you through several prompts to encourage introspection and extract meaning from your practice of making connections with the outside world and your perception.

Allow yourself to be animated by these cues.

As they arise in the body, heart, mind, memory, imagination, and sense of belonging, feel each one of them.

Give them time to simmer.

Allow what binds you to the world to come to light.

Don't merely pause for introspection; start a dialogue with the people you live with.

- How does a practice of a body origin story manifest in your experience?
- Why is the body considered a seed of communities?
- What kind of stories begin to grow within you?

To listen to this practice, follow the link yuriacelidwen.com
or the QR code on the table of contents.

9

Senshine

IN THE GLOBALIZED world, hyperindividuality and reliance on brain processes have become the model of being. Meanwhile, our relationship with our bodies is interrelated with our minds, and our relationality with each other and Mother Earth is continuously dismissed and undermined. To flourish and recover our embodied homes requires healing from this alienation. It requires counteractions of connection and belonging.

> When mud is exposed to the Sun
> not only fades its darkness
> but loses its thickness
> lighter as into dust it dissolves

Reclaiming the brightness of our senses holds the possibility of this taking place. I call this particular form of contemplation *senshine*. *Senshine* is a playful coming together of "senses" and "sunshine"—the joy of the senses and the brightness of the sunshine. It reminds us to look at how our full experience—heart, imagination, memory, reason, sound, sight, touch, smell, and taste—brightens our sensitivity to life. *Senshine* nurtures the observation of direct experience as a source of traditional wisdom.

> Thick layers of ice and silence bring the tree to its knees,
> surrendering its branches to the winds.
> Unyielding, the roots expand firm,
> knowing of their unfaltering dignity,
> despite the poison in the soil.

They know of the stories of their Ancestors' seeds.
We are all the seed, the tree, and the branch
ragged from the broad trunk of community.

We are the wounded, our sapwood exposed,
our inner ripped bark broken, our inner threads left hanging.
We are the silent stump, stunned, turned to numbness.
Contemplation awakens us to such fragility
and to our miraculous resilience.

Indigenous People from many different traditions have come together to recreate a collective identity, an international identity of unity and plurality. I am confident this model can integrate non-Indigenous Peoples and communities with each other and our Lands so that we all identify as part of the Mother Earth system. Lands are crucial to establishing a sense of collective belonging to the planet.

The Indigenous movement has proved that sharing challenges can inspire people to come together, celebrating the richness of the diverse points of view to bring together a community goal for planetary flourishing. However, it is impossible to imagine a community with no equity of presence and power of decision. To get to that place, there must be the possibility of speaking one on one with respect, a sense of love, and through myriad languages, embodied forms, not only through words.

Aren't we all tired of broken treaties, broken words, promises that lead to nothing? We want action, communal participatory action, planetary partnerships to bring to the fore true action for equity, justice, and love for planetary societies. We are at a moment when we must stop talking about the narrow perspective of "human flourishing" and embrace its broader lens of planetary flourishing first. There are no human health determinants if there are no planetary health determinants. We must address our entire Earth community, bringing the richness and plurality of voices.

I regard the concept of "Oneness" as an essentialist interpretation of holistic nihilism. It is a hasty and, to be honest, extremely cowardly escape.

It alludes to a process or existence devoid of purpose or significance. Holistic nihilism ignores and erases the horrific atrocities done to other living beings while falling for the flimsy notion that we are all one. It also profoundly misunderstands the diversity of relationships, contexts, and the principle of kin relationality. Rather than pushing for a uniform manner of being, we can learn from the global Indigenous movement to regard our distinctiveness and use that richness to orient toward a shared goal.

The wise women of the Misak Peoples, from the Putumayo district in the southern part of Colombia within the Amazon rainforest, come from a long lineage of weaver masters who incorporate their cosmology in the weaving of baskets. Theirs is a practice that involves all sensory experiences. Their weaving arts establish moral codes, weaving joy, goodness, meaning, and wellness in the community.

These ethical, aesthetic arts are excellent examples of *senshine*. Weaving is not only a metaphor for our interrelatedness but also an action, a practice, a contemplative way to generate insight on what we bring to the world and how we do it. Every thread, warp, and weft interlaces moral beauty in the actions of the body, heart, and mind in service of Spirit. Echoes of the Misak weaving tradition are found in communities worldwide.

Approaching contemplation through this lens, expanding from a familiar home ground of Mother Earth to the seed of the body and further into sensorial nuance, leads to a granular alertness of unfolding experience. It is *contemplative flourishing as a path of truth and connection*.

Like the Misak Peoples, we must own our experience through our senses to reveal a shining world. We must dive into how triggered memories color our narratives and distort our direct experience—like a broken thread that's lost its fabric and may need the most careful tending to be gently weaved back to the whole. When this happens, we must practice transparent perception, letting our senses be porous to the world's luminosity. Our senses will shine through as we unite not in uniformity but in distinctive plurality, where each thread gives the whole strength, structure, and beauty.

Senshine and Animic Entities

To this day, Nahua Mesoamerican traditions draw on a system of body essences called animic entities documented from precontact times before colonialism was imposed upon their Lands.[1] Nahua animic entities are forms of subtle energy that motivate action and give life to a person's dispositions, character traits, emotions, and temperaments. They set in motion and incite behavior. Since they inhabit the body, they influence sensations, embodiment, and enaction. Contemplation on the influence of these entities is another form of senshine.

In the Nahua body system, the senses are seats of consciousness that hold the power of decision-making, will, and creative force, and thus of temperance, attention, and flow. When observed, embraced, and allowed to flow intentionally, the subtle energies moving through the body may encourage balance, well-being, and flourishing. However, when exacerbated, these energies may lead to confusion, reactivity, and devastation. Nahua communities use various practices of observation, regulation, and channeling of these energies.

An eminent quality of these systems is that afflictions are systemic. As we often see within Indigenous lifeways, humans are never separated from Nature. Humans belong to the whole and so we influence, stimulate, and are shaped by the environment. In the same way, animic entities are never solely human. They may manifest in the body, heart, and mind, but they are informed by disturbances in the environment where the flow of Spirit has been hindered.

The animic entities are thought to traverse the world in multiple realms. These dimensions vary only in degree of subtlety. They can leave the body and inhabit other bodies temporarily. Therefore, one way to restore the natural flow, health, and flourishing in the ecosystem is to tend to these entities. By embracing them fully, we do not resist but instead open to new tides for the flow of essences to run in a beneficial sway.

The animic entities embody a fun and bewildering plethora of sense manifestations. What an exquisite form of senshine! In the Nahuatl language, the senses are called *tonematia* or *tonemachiliz* (the spelling and words may vary from region to region, given the development of the language variations over centuries of local influences). The words are related to *nematiliztli*, which indicates sentience, wisdom, and moral virtues such as truthfulness, compassion, courage, and kindness.[2] I venture that these entities may be the seat of our belonging to the world. They are the core of being in the world through meaning and purpose.

Since these animic entities are how we get to know the world, they are also known as *ontlamatiliztli*, which translates to "where the world is felt or known" as a location, whether a realm of earth or of experience. They are also known as *totlahuelmatia,* or "our enjoyers of the world," as vehicles or vessels of aesthetic experiences such as beauty, joy, awe, bliss, and reverence.

There are yet other ways to exemplify the senshine of experience, and they include the following:

Taste, or *tlayeyecoliztli,* is the action of coming to know the world, and *tlacamayeyecoliztli* is the action of savoring through the mouth. Imagine this sense as an intimate way to be taken over by the feeling of nourishment. Doesn't it offer a spicy variety of flavors? Then imagine that the taste becomes part of each cell of your body suddenly opening your pores as if your whole skin were in awe, widely opening to take in the joy of tasting, feeling the gush of life through the body—or, hopefully not too often, halting it in disgust. Taste and savoring, *tlayeyecoliztli* and *tlacamayeyecoliztli,* have claimed you. You have seasoned the world—even *become* the world in savor!

Tlachializtli and *teittaliztli* are the act of meeting the world through sight and divining or perceiving by intuition. The act of seeing is understood as occurring not only through the eyes but also through insight. Envision then that our senses are subtle ways to perceive even the invisible realities, which pass unnoticed to mere eyes. How much are we missing when we go through the trails of life distracted? The love of our lives may have just passed by when we were walking asleep.

The act of listening with the heart, which is very related to active listening, is *tlacaquiliztli.* It also means "mind" and the most essential part of the soul, where the art of comprehension crafts ingenuity. This is the natural force that allows for wisdom and judgment. I wonder how the world would be if our justice systems were not based on models of retribution, in which deterrence provides the groundwork for maintaining order and punishment is proportional to the crime committed? Instead, what if justice were based on collective needs attended to from the momentous comprehension of the causes and conditions for collective flourishing? In such a system, solutions would be based on the needs of the world's soul.

Smell is the act of recognizing the world, or *totlanecuia*, and shares with *totlanequia* "will" and "volition" as acting willfully, wanting, and consenting. It hints at how becoming familiar with the world relies on our approaching it with the volition of relating with it and recognizing our kinship with the world in a fully embodied experience. It is as if both the world and we were consenting to each other's transformation in the exchange.

Tlamatocaya is the caresser of reality, or touch, the exchange, expression, and dissemination of care and affection. Loving, caressing touch is vital for flourishing kin, for its remarkable relational cradle of safety allows for vulnerability in its reciprocal quality. A lack of touch has been shown to decrease overall wellness, and even those who intentionally avoid closeness and value autonomy show flourishing benefits from touch.[3] There is so much we must learn about how to touch appropriately. It is well known that allogrooming, or social grooming, is shared by many of our more-than-human mammal Relatives.[4] For example, more-than-human primates spend almost a quarter of their day grooming one another for health and social benefits, principally to reinforce social structures and bonds and to enhance the immune system.[5] Similarly, research has found that rats whose mothers frequently lick and groom them when they are infants grow up showing reduced fear and anxiety, more curiosity for novelty, and more resilience to stress, with stronger immune systems.[6]

Certain organs of the body, the *totlatecoaca*, are considered seats of the senses that carry out our will. For instance, the navel is the seat of dignity that connects with the external world; the mouth holds the word, the prayer, and the song; the lips and tongue give way to gentle and poetic speech; the throat is the dwelling of the voice; the fingers are the vehicle of visual expression; and the feet allow us to roam the body of Mother Earth.

There are three main seats of animic entities for the Nahua: the *tonalli* in the head, the *teyolía* in the heart, and the *ihíyotl* in the liver. The faculties of experience go from cognition to instinct and passion, with a particular emphasis on the convergence of experience in the heart as the center of the body, where meaning and purpose are generated. The higher transcendent states are said to happen through the confluence of the senses in the heart, not above in the head nor below in the liver.

The *tonalli*, or vital force, is situated in the whole head, but its energy is concentrated prominently in the crown and is associated with rational thinking and consciousness. This subtle energy interacts directly with the world and ultimately continues through rebirth. It nourishes the flavors of experience and receives the *kinam*, or personal heat; the *k'awil*, or ancestral energy of lineage; and the *óol*, or breath that wanders during sleep. The *teyolía* in the heart is the seat of the experience of vitality, knowledge, inclinations, habits, predispositions, memory, will, emotion, and affection, all of which orient action. It is considered the most important of the three main entities. In the Maya tradition, the *teyolía* is also known as the *bat'tz'il ch'ulel* or *mutil o'tan*, the bird of the heart that can leave the body temporarily to visit the houses of memories, dreams, and poetry. The *ihíyotl* situated in the liver processes and digests the impulses and passions of the body. It internalizes and integrates experience and is the most related to basic bodily functions.

How the three seats play and influence one another gives way to nuances of experience. For example, when the heart is heavily influenced by the *ihíyotl* (liver), the seat of tranquility and pleasure, the sensory experience will have a tone of consolation or satiation. If, to the contrary, the heart is influenced by the *tonalli* (head), then it will lean toward contemplation and insight. In experiences of wholeness, communion, or transcendence—such as love and grief, bliss and awe—the three animic entities are in full participation, within and without. This is the full senshine experience.

Senshine and Collective Flourishing

Feeling dis-membered is the result of human othering, of cultural narratives that disconnect us from our senses, our body seeds, and the grove of the Earth community. The separation tears us apart and gets in the way of belonging. This yearning sets us on a journey of discovery.

On the lookout for home—for familiarity, vulnerability, and intimacy—we surrender to a swollen cloud of unknowing. We ever-so-slowly distill drops of joy and meaning out of direct experience. We re-member. We expand sense-making to relationships between the body and other bodies and the Land. We relate to the Land as a way to connect us. We wake to the bliss of presence. We become Spirit. It is the senses that reveal Spirit in the body.

A yearning for connection runs deep in our bones. It is a roaring thunder and a burning lightning unleashing gusts of panic, the origins of which are too far behind to recall. It is a limb that has been severed and we only now realize we once had it. Its absence left a ghost.

Our path from the acorn to the grove—from narrow self-interest to expansive participation in the generative community—requires that we acknowledge the conditions of our sociocultural landscapes and intentionally transform them. While retaining some cultural conditions is necessary to navigate the norms and expectations of social participation, reifying or keeping them fixed limits our capacity to create new conditions and stories.

I encourage you to investigate how culture flavors our significance and our purpose.

Contemplation generates insight into the creation of cultural norms through narratives. Our narratives can and should be questioned and intentionally amended. Established narratives of supremacy must be composted to give rise to new, collaborative ways of being and knowing. We can let go of the cultural narratives that prevent us from connecting to ourselves and others. We can open to our senses to form new personal and cultural narratives that can orient us through new, familiar, and foreign environments. We can create new shared stories of interdependence and belonging, of collective flourishing.

Three contemplative insights are crucial for such a path of creation. The first is a reckoning of our dis-membering.

Dis-memberment

We must acknowledge the human othering of self, others, and Mother Earth, and consider how we perceive such threats through our sensory experience.

Grounding the senses on the body seed and on the body of Mother Earth elicits an awareness of Spirit and how it flows, the relentless impact of phenomena sharing and receiving. These energy flows, ever in motion through the senses, form the self with the body as the container of individual identity. However, when identity narratives become too rigid, the sense of self becomes inflated, separating it from the community. Dis-memberment explores the search for the self in our very disconnected age through the metaphor of the body. As gates of experience, the senses are mirrors on which memory labels meaning, and then action and intention reveal wisdom.

Stories are intentional constructs. They give us an identity, a place, a purpose, and inspire us to action. They are necessary to achieve specific goals for the social collective, but they are not absolutes. Othering results from stories of erasure, from the groups in power deciding what stories to tell. Othering narratives impact humans, more-than-humans, and our shared home, Mother Earth. For example, the othering stories of Euro-American colonialism imposed identities of separation, alienation, dehumanization, and doubt upon Indigenous Peoples, our Lands, Territories, and resources. The central characteristic of these stories was an othering of Indigenous identities in an attempt to usurp our Lands, to destroy our exceptional bond with our Territories. They led to our invasion, persecution, marginalization, exploitation, and commodification. They inspired the violation of our bodies and our Lands.

These othering narratives can be traced back to the Doctrine of Discovery, to foundational documents, royal charters, papal bulls, and ideas of manifest destiny.[7] They continue to promote separatist, geno-cidal, and ecocidal dogmas through legislation, Land regulation, and education. Discrimination based on identity bias continues to perpet-uate structural systems of violence and stories of othering. Mocking and ridicule, denial, nationalism, and narratives of exceptionalism continue to appear in religious beliefs, assimilation plans, and every-day language.

Let us hold ourselves accountable for the horrors of our time, *and* let us have the courage to face these stories and ideologies that feed our dis-memberment.

We embody the shock, fear, and brutality evoked by threats to the body as a limb of community. We acknowledge the fragility of existence and accept that this harm leads to psychologically unnerving conclusions.

We take the millennia of othering stories of colonialism, coloniality, and oppression, the rooted historical causes of cultural genocide, and the impacts of narratives of inadequacy and disempowerment—and we compost them. We let them decay.

We let them become pure awareness for a new shared spiritual story. We re-member.

Re-membering

The art of re-membering—growing new branches and sprouting new seedlings—recreates and reenvisions belonging. It gives the sense of an ever-expansive circle of care for Mother Earth, that we are part of the communities that make this shared home planet. A practice of sensory experience directly reveals all of our collective input. As gates of expe-rience, the senses are mirrors on which memory labels meaning, and then action and intention reveal wisdom. Through this practice of re-membering, we aspire to integrate the senses into action.

Re-membering happens when the elements—Fire, Water, Air, Earth, Skies, and Heart—gather in a mixture of humus and sod, peat and kindness. This fertilizer is a practice of reckoning. It is a continuous, meticulous examination and acknowledgment of the stories by which we live. It requires investigating the conditions, causes, and impact of created and recreated narratives with vulnerability and openness.

The origin stories of the Nahua and Maya peoples we contemplated earlier remind us of the beginning place of turmoil and agitation and its potential for transformation into order. Today's world and the overwhelming strains upon Mother Earth, chaotic as it is, is pregnant with reorientation opportunities. There is so much potential for intentional compassionate action and participation.

Indigenous Peoples' Day is reclaiming its place over the historic enslavement and genocide of Native Peoples in Turtle Island and Abya Yala. With statues of Columbus, missionaries like Junipero Serra, and other historical figures being taken down around the country, the status quo is being challenged.[8] Narratives of othering are being recreated—re-membered through narratives of belonging, through the seeds of order.

In the process of transforming narratives, the international Indigenous movement has successfully re-membered distinct multiethnic identities—shared globally by five thousand different Nations in ninety countries—to intentionally create shared platforms of participation through horizontal and democratic structures.

The movement has found agreement within our plurality in our shared care for our larger community: care for other living beings and care for Mother Earth. Now as political actors on the global stage, we are growing in our power to change policies, to advance the demands of equity and justice for Mother Earth.

We are re-membering ourselves with our Earth community, our flourishing kin.

Re-membering comes from recreating action values of gratitude, responsibility, and belonging to community and from re-wilding us and the natural world. We are recovering languages, practices, and beliefs.

Indigenous cosmovisions are also guiding new ways of being. Using Traditional Ecological Knowledge (TEK), we are contributing to ecological recovery and conservation in relationships, models of diversity, and the integration of an intentional common goal for justice and equity. This environmental work is intentional community work that re-members the limbs of the world.

Becoming Spirit

Indigenous ways of being and forms of contemplation center on cultivating flourishing human-Mother Earth relationships. Our worldviews go beyond the individual in an aspirational self-transcendent process. Our everyday practices manifest in how our senses shine through—how we perceive, relate, and respond to the world.

Our contemplative flourishing is our path of truth and connection.

Awe arises from sensitivity to the natural world and expressing its relationships—by sharing stories of moral splendor and aesthetic expression, rituals of collective effervescence, and transcendent experiences of communion, primordial transitions, and revelations.[9] A humble regard for these exceptional relational capacities pushes the self toward a communal experience of kin relationality, where Spirit reveals itself as all-pervading. We *become* the experience of Spirit itself.

In other words, kin relationality, our love for others and Mother Earth, creates a participatory planetary system that aids in our collective Spiritual becoming.

Spirit is as diverse as the names and characteristics of creation.

It is *Akongo*, "the Mysterious One," among the Ngombe Peoples of the Congo, the supreme source of being, a beautifully imagined everlasting forest.

On Turtle Island, it is conceived as a "Great Spirit Mystery" in *Wakan Tanka*, the supreme Creator of the Sioux; or the *Kitchi Manitou*, whose generosity and mercy keep life going among the Ojibway.

It is *Ometeotl*, the primordial deity, nondual in its characteristics and encompassing all possibilities, among the Nahuas of Mesoamerica. Or *Viracocha* in the Andes, formed by all aspects of creation, the beginning of light.

It is the primeval force of life in the Babylonian *Tiamat*, the sea of formless creation and potential.

Ogdoad in ancient Egypt encompasses all the energy of the primeval tangle of chaos and is represented as coupled deities merged in all the possibilities and opportunities about to arise.

Ymir the Norse rose to life at the conciliation of fire and ice and is dismembered to give life to creation.

Tane, the Maori forest deity, rises from the union of Papa Skies and Rangi Mother Earth, who succeeded in causing the generative space where life can grow.

Ta'aroa in Tahiti is the "Unique One," the supreme creator of life through dismembering and offering his body as a source.

These understandings, though diverse, all see Spirit as encompassing material creation and subtle elemental landscapes. They differ from Western theological perspectives that often contrast Spirit and matter. The Hebrew *ru'a*—divine breath—sees Spirit as a divine inspiration.[10] The ancient Greeks understood it as *pneuma*, the breath of life, separating it from the psyche or mind.[11] (Aristotle's hylomorphic doctrine, however, argued for an embodied breath or ensouled body, in which soul is the first principle of animal life.[12]) The Christian term *mens* indicates that Spirit, as mind or thought, is unique to humans but different from a soul, while other interpretations saw Spirit as synonymous with the soul but distinct from the body.[13]

Contemporary scientific attempts to approach Spirit point to a perspective similar to the Indigenous one: Spirit as a primordial embodiment of the imminent creative force present in all forms of life and phenomena. In physics, this representation is reflected in chaos theory as well as concepts like autopoiesis and complexity. The tension between these apparent opposites—order and chaos, knowing and not knowing—is necessary for creation to arise.

As my Elders used to say, living the spiral path entails leaving a seat at the table for the trickster. In other words, we must embrace the surprise, the stillness, and the unwavering change. We must let the unknown unfold.

My Ancestors' practice was one of holding the rainbows and the storms. Such keen observations have offered a map to sense, to traverse Landscapes *outward* in place, space, and time and *inward* in the body, dreams, and imaginations.

The equinox:
apparent cessation
the pause of impossible balance.
Full of awe, its elusive cosmic dance.
As above, so below:
although none is,
but equanimity.

As participants and creators of community we preserve life as it is *and* become Spirit in its primordial infinite multiplicity and potentiality. We aspire to moment-to-moment experiences of intentional collective care *and* action. We attempt to hold the rainbows and the storms.

PRACTICE

Senshine

Indigenous forms of contemplation arouse compassion the way rain gives rise to petrichor. Apart from encouraging our wish to alleviate suffering in others and ourselves, Indigenous contemplation advances an examination of how environmental balance has been lost and how it can be regained through skillful action. When done communally, this meditative, gentle engagement catalyzes accountability for harm and the humility of unwavering commitment to the dignity and integrity of life.

We have explored how Indigenous rituals and ceremonies incorporate the shine of the senses, giving them familiarity and relatability.

Furthermore, we have contemplated how to retell our own narratives for connection, inclusion, and belonging.

Now, we will bring forth the senshine experience, a joy of the senses in aesthetic arrest, an awe-induced stilling of the mind. Aesthetic absorption cultivates curiosity and self-transcendence. Through this practice of sensory contemplation on inter- and intracultural expressions, we build together toward collective effervescence.

While acknowledging the benefits of the Western mindfulness movement, let's look into the blind spots of practices that center a Western individualist ideal. What has been the result? What is at risk? What are we missing?

Recall that this approach follows the steps of introspection, recollection, and insight. During the first inner visualization, you are invited to take a first trip to your senses, extending all the way back to a source of bare truth of experience.

Maybe this serves as a starting point for a conversation about the interactive relationship between your senses, body, and world. Your senses become the very pulp from which stories are sculpted. They are anchored in the present by your connection to your environment. This encounter offers you a new perspective on how you sense the world.

You are welcome to participate in an outdoor practice during the exploratory phase.

As your senses arise in the body, heart, mind, memory, imagination, and sense of belonging, feel each one of them.

Pause

Make sure your electronics are off or put them somewhere else if you haven't already.

Locate a comfortable location nearby.

Sit outside in the natural surroundings if the weather permits. If not, pick a location that lets you take in the scenery.

Make the location you've chosen easily accessible. Ideally, your daily routine should allow you to access your practice from anywhere at any time.

Let your body rest in a way that helps you stay relaxed but attentive.

Treat yourself with kindness and refrain from going too far beyond your comfort zone. This is the standard procedure for any practice you come across. The journey should be calm enough to make you feel safe yet encourage you to keep going forward and inward, gradually and kindly, one step closer, connecting.

Pause

Move from imagination to experience. Practice a form of collective contemplation. Our community is all phenomena in and around.

Establish first the container of the web of relationships of Mother Earth. Bring these relationships into the body through the senses.

Visit the kin-relational aspects of being part of a system of beings. Our Lakota Relatives wisely say *Mitákuye Oyás'iŋ*: all Our Relations and move gradually observing the dialogue of lived experience.

Approach the present moment as the source of experience. Realize experience as the source of tradition.

All times are here, right now.

Our lineages of the past are here, in the actions of our present, for the benefit of those to come.

All right here, in this very present precious moment of awareness.

How is Spirit manifesting through your experience right now?

How is this experience revealing the Spirit of the Lands and the Spirit of our Ancestors?

Sensory experience generates ways of being and ways of knowing, but how?

How are these ways expressed?

Spirit lives in the stories, artistic expressions, sources of sensory perception.

What are the senses saying of the world around?

Is there a beginning and end point of your senses and the world around you?

Or is it that they all appear continuous?

How do we respond to the world? How does the world influence us?

Where is each sense located in the body? Are there any that feel more active, as the Nahua Peoples suggest? Is it above toward the head? Or below toward the liver? Are they converging in the heart?

Investigate the responses and drives elicited by the senses.

Is there pleasure? Or revulsion?

How are you responding to what is? Encounter experience in its fullness. Don't try to make sense of them. Let the experience be direct. Let's start.

Open

How readily the breath aligns to the crisp clarity of the senses.

The piercing senses make the breath more porous,
more profound,

e x p a n s i v e

Are the senses making the breath more present?

The breath responds,
becoming more natural.

Riding the waves of the senses, the breath.

It flows and dissipates as the senses respond to phenomena around.

The vastness of space and the richness of the senses stretch the breath.
They make it more flexible.
The breath now swells.

Eases.

It finds its ground,
Its presence,
its place through the senses.

Allow the breath to lose bondages,
all constrictions, all obstacles,
slowly let them dissolve,
let them go.

Sail in ease the waves of the senses.

Body, mind, heart, and senses

Present

The spaciousness of the breath and the senses permeate every cell
in your body.

The tongue in every pore bursts in awe . . .

O p e n

Present .

In relation

In experience

In the body

Right here

Right now

Present

The breath, the senses, the heart, and the body
become intimate with experience in this present moment.
Be curious of what is within, flowing, communicating, relating.
Let anything that comes arise.

Observe the body, letting go of tension and resistance to what is
around and
within.

Letting anything new become familiar.
Maybe it had been here before.
Maybe you are just now noticing.

Very gently pass over your body.
Notice what is weaving with these areas that make them respond so.

Let attention now sweetly caress the senses.

Softly let go . . .

In the Quest for Insight

You are guided by a few cues in your quest for insight to deepen your introspection and reveal more about your relationship with your senses.

Allow yourself to be animated by these cues.

Give them time to simmer.

Allow what binds you to the world to come to light. Continue your pursuit of understanding beyond introspection. If it is still feasible and safe for you to do so, extend an invitation to speak with those with whom you shared Lands as home. If not, learning about the Lands and their changing nature can help you form a closer bond with them.

Take part in learning from the Lands themselves about the Lands. Next, carry on the discussion with those who, among the Lands' own inhabitants, both human and non-human, have contributed to the Lands' ability to express themselves.

- How is flowing from conversing intimately with your breath, senses, heart, and body in this present moment?

- What is reaching to you trying to communicate and relate?

- Is there any tension or resistance? Where may the source of the resistance be?

- Take a moment and in whatever way that feels appropriate let your experience be conveyed aesthetically. In other words, let it be sublimated in some form of art.

To listen to this practice, follow the link yuriacelidwen.com
or the QR code on the table of contents.

10

Heartful Wisdom

OUR CONTEMPLATIVE INQUIRY in *Flourishing Kin* has traversed from *kin relationality* as the web of life to the *body seed* and how it dialogues with inner and outer phenomena and into the *senshine* experience. This path suggests how living beings originate and nourish from their ecosystem and transform and decay to sustain the shared extensive networks. In this chapter we are flowing into the heart.

The Indigenous heart sings of the actions of love: the composting of self-centered perceptions and the regeneration of compassion and care practices for humans *and* non-human beings.

From the Mesoamerican perspective, the heart is the central animic entity weaving through all experiences. It is the seat of our emotions. Emotions here are the spiritual, interrelated forces or systems of impulses that offer opportunities for prosocial behaviors. In the social sciences, prosocial behavior relates to interpersonal, social acts that benefit or care for other humans. Here, I suggest an expanded definition that calls for radical actions of belonging based on love for all beings.

A prosocial self-construct or idea of self is the bedrock of Indigenous contemplative spiritualities and sciences. The Indigenous zeal for kinship sets the ground for relationality, mutuality, collaboration, and shared life. Traversing kin relationality, let us consider the idea of the social self through emotions—within our systems of relationships and our myriad symbolic artistic expressions.

It is well accepted that mind and culture are mutually constituted and socially constructed.[1] In the last two decades, emotions have also gained prominence as crucial motivators of behavior, establishing them as a substratum of culture.[2] Emotions can engender othering (when exclusive) or belonging (when intentionally prosocial). Emotions can also be the channel for exceptional artistic expression.[3] Emotional artistry resonates in Indigenous communication patterns, responses, and expressions. Each song of emotional experience or symphony of constellations of emotions points to our prosocial values and collaborations among different species within local ecologies. We use Indigenous stories of empowerment, where regulation and orientation of emotional impulses generate better interactions and actions toward collective well-being, to support practices of care and belonging within our Mother Earth communities.

Today, however, climate and health pandemics seem to be causing an emotional recession that makes finding the heart increasingly tricky. Heart disturbances, from grief to moral injury, manifest as languishing through anxiety and depression, sadness, guilt and shame, anger and fear.[4] Climate devastation has caused a context-specific ailment called eco-grief or *solastalgia*, the existential distress caused by the climate crisis.[5] As opposed to nostalgia—the homesickness felt when separated from home—*solastalgia* is the distress of *being connected* to home and realizing its degradation. It manifests as dislocation, helplessness, and a loss of purpose from being undermined by forces destroying the potential for solace.

Meek public policies on climate action and political and economic-based decisions—like the US not being a signatory of the Convention on Biological Diversity—intensify heart grief and stress from a lack of influence and control on our life conditions.[6] These power dynamics impede down-regulation and a return to emotional baseline, further impacting collective well-being. However, a change in cultural narratives can lead to social empowerment. Instead of our old cultural origin stories of exploitation, oppression, and abuse, which reinforce human supremacy, let us rewrite our stories to reflect ecological values that restore our Mother Earth system with the aim of collective flourishing.

Youth are especially vulnerable to these disturbances of the heart, falling prey to feelings of alienation, confusion, and disconnection from the principles and contexts of community. The global rise in depression and anxiety during and post-pandemic weighs significantly on youth, especially girls.[7] Such forms of languishing in the last decade are related to technological dependency, poor peer relationships, decreased parental presence and nurturance, and increased parental rejection.[8]

These extreme forms of heart grief result in increased suicidal ideation and attempts. My own experience with self-harm as a young person is shared with an upsetting 14 to 20 percent of young adults. Adding to the collective wounds is the heartbreaking fact that teen survivors of sexual abuse have an increased likelihood of suicide, hostility, high-risk behavior, post-traumatic stress disorder (PTSD), and major depressive disorders (MDD). I know this story all too well in my flesh.

For everyone, especially youth, learning to find hope through resilience is now more critical than ever. Indigenous metaphors, songs, and collective movement (dance and ritual) reflect an unreserved kinship with our more-than-human Relatives. To know a phenomenon through its environmental interactions is to realize the complexity and plurality of Mother Earth and its kin relational quality. These brushstrokes of more nuanced outer and inner relational processes encourage an experiential sense of belonging, an essential looking outward for planetary health. They are the precursors to practices of compassion and care for flourishing kin.

Recent studies define compassion as the awareness of suffering of self and others, assessing the causes and conditions of such suffering, and the will to alleviate it. I want to emphasize the aspect of love action missing in this Western taxonomy. Compassion is action-oriented; it results in loving interventions intended to alleviate sorrow. Compassion also features mutuality; that is, the intervention transforms both entities. Compassion is not hierarchical as in benefactor-beneficiary. It is horizontal. The love action transforms all entities involved and connects them in fuller ways.

Thus, compassion is a profoundly moving emotional experience of self and others. In this way, it is not too distinct from an aesthetic arrest, an awe-filled stilling of the mind in the presence of great beauty. When we witness suffering, it causes us to reckon with our impermanence and our relationality. We recognize the same emotional experiences that occur in self and others. We assess their pain as our own. And we are motivated to alleviate such pain—to transform languishing into flourishing—and to participate in the care that benefits and connects all beings of Mother Earth, including all environmental phenomena.

For Indigenous Peoples, compassion enhances our actions of love and belonging for our flourishing kin. The song of our heart is one of bliss. It is a liberating, active, and creative force reaching ever closer to flourishing, enabling resilience, adaptation, and resourcefulness.

Heartfelt Wisdom and Collective Flourishing

How can knowledge lead to actions that meet the challenges of our times: social and environmental injustices, health disparities, mass incarceration, and environmental destruction? Indigenous contemplative traditions have long sought to cultivate embodied and action-oriented knowledge. Heartfelt wisdom honors this goal. It encourages a shift from survival responses and intergenerational trauma toward care, connection, resilience, and flourishing. It builds on the prosocial values of reverence, respect, accountability, responsibility, kindness, generosity, awe, love, and sacredness.

We reflect on the heart as the seat of emotions and how they orient us toward collaboration and participatory actions for collective flourishing. We explore the colonial domination of Mother Earth and how it has impacted Indigenous Peoples and People of Color worldwide. Finally, as we move toward regeneration and planetary flourishing, we contemplate ways to build on our empowerment and resilience to enhance flourishing kin.

Here, we go deeper into prosocial behavior and how humans are prone to cultivate kind, social, and collaborative communities when exposed to diversified systems of being and knowing. Collective well-being centers on pluralism. It requires respect and esteem for cultural voices across lines of divergence and even conflict.

Conflict is part of learning how to be human. Conflict is present in, out, and through the human experience. When we ignore this reality, we have difficulties moving forward. We must accept that our worldviews may differ to encourage a critical view. We must assume they may contrast significantly with those deprived of language, culture, and Lands. Thus, we must turn our hearts to listen to their songs.

Indigenous traditions worldwide emphasize community well-being through kin relationality. This cultural value of prosocial emotions and behavior is vital for building resilient and flourishing communities of care and trust. We cultivate virtues and moral qualities through contemplative practices that embrace emotional vulnerability; individual concentration and equanimity; consideration of our place and impact on others' well-being through observation and regulation of ourselves, others, and our interactions; and collective presence against oppressive cultural systems through engaged communities of transformative love, equity, and just action.

PRACTICE

Heartful Wisdom

This practice takes the path of the heart to contain all beings with their multiple and habitually contradictory emotions. By doing so, the illusion of separation can be reoriented toward acceptance, forgiveness, and even love. We aspire to nurture our natural loving superpowers to care for our integrated plural Mother Earth system. Learning how to love expansively means caring for ourselves first. Only when we have learned to care for ourselves can we fruitfully turn to others.

According to this practice, loving is forgiveness but not endorsing or exposing ourselves to harm. The work entails acknowledging our limitations, committing to seeing them clearly to overcome them, and trusting others to do their inner work. However, completely give up expecting that others will. As part of our love commitment, we have confidence in people to make their own decisions about the kind of life they want and the direction and pace of their development. Otherwise, we may very well fall into condescension, which is as off-putting as disgust. To effectively help ourselves and others, we must first emerge from the maze of our own conflicting emotions, especially in cases where we have experienced abuse.

Empowering heartful wisdom entails releasing ourselves from such entanglements and garden emotions by composting them, pruning them, and letting new ones bloom.

Like previous practices, this one brings into being songs of the heart in the present moment. These songs will sing of wise relationality. The practice invites a dialogue with the simultaneous contradictory assortment of emotions. We recognize their affective influence and orient the force toward loving care.

Emotions shape our identity based on cosmic relationships through the heart of experience. It is in the heart where the act of relating meets plurality and communion and becomes love.

The first part of this practice encourages you to delve into present exploration and observation of emotions. In the second part, following the emotions without labeling allows you to explore the intuitive aspects of an interactive conversation with emotions

Don't anticipate a single outcome.

Permit yourself to feel how the practice affects and changes you.

Turn off your devices or put them elsewhere if you haven't done so already.

Locate a spot where you are comfortable.

Make the location you've chosen accessible. Ideally, your practice should be available daily, anywhere at any time.

Allow your muscles to relax in a manner that guarantees your focus and ease.

No matter where you are, pay attention to how your emotions manifest and change.

The path should be gradual, gentle, and soothing yet encourage us to move little by little beyond our comfort zone.

Pause

Settling in the body with our eyes closed,
we go after the texture of our heart.
We follow the light of attention, illuminating emotions in the heart.

Aware of emotions.
They rise, heighten, dissipate,
shifting, fluctuating, and ever-changing throughout the heart.

Heart is body.
Body is heart.
Sentient of emotions.

Parallel emotions, plentiful emotions,
sometimes, opposite emotions at once.
A present heart listens, tends, and opens.

Body and heart are aware: in pure presence.
Fluid, porous, transient,
emotions flow through a crescent heart.

Each is distinct, yet together,
mended, restored, are whole:
a heart of hearts in presence.

A fluid flow of presence in the heart becomes water
running through the body, becomes air
running through the breath, becomes fire
running through action, becomes earth
running though reverence, aware of Spirit
here and now,
the heart embraces all without demand.

Slow heart, gentle flow, tender presence,
a warm fire caresses infinite life in our heart of light
a heart of light and presence,
a heart of light and care,
a heart of light and Earth and Skies and Spirit.

Heart touches the ground beneath the feet.
Grateful heart for the Earth,
grateful heart for the Skies.

Place your hands to your throat:
speech of heart in silence and voice.

Place your hands to your forehead:
mind of heart in thoughts, memories, and imagination.

Place your hands on your heart:
actions of an endless torrent of care for one whole heart of life.

Inhale and lift the heart to speak one word of love today.
Exhale slowly, and start opening your eyes.

In the Quest for Insight

This quest for insight will guide you through a few cues to further reflect and elicit insight into your emotions and how they impact your world.

Let these cues animate your experience. Feel each of them as they rise in the body, heart, mind, memory, imagination, and belonging.

Let them simmer.

Let what connects you to the world emerge.

Do not stop in the quest for insight only in self-reflection but invite a conversation with those with whom you share your life.

This practice took the path of emotions and the way they orient behavior and relationships. It encourages a conversation with your emotions, not a projection of assumptions nor expectations of what they are or should be.

In the first explorative part of the practice, you are invited to ponder how emotions color our perception of the world. While these colored views may be helpful, they can also become obstacles to our genuine relationship with the world around us.

- Describe what emotions are in your own words.

- How do emotions manifest today, and how do I identify them since many happen simultaneously?

- What do emotions say about my life, surroundings, and relationships?

- In what ways are emotions helpful and in what ways obstacles?

- How can the practice help me in conversing with my emotions and those of others?

To listen to this practice, follow the link yuriacelidwen.com or the QR code on the table of contents.

11

Ecological Belonging

THE MAYA PEOPLES call it *Ut'z Kaslemaj*, the ethics and arts of encouraging the recovery, protection, and transmission of the ancestral practice of living well with Mother Earth.[1] *Suma Kawsay* is the art of living well and ethically in Andean regions. For the Haudenosaunee, collective force strength or power from intention and enaction is known as *Kasasten'sera*.[2] The Warlpiri Peoples of Northern Australia's Tanami Desert call the all-encompassing ethical system that guides an integrated way of life through morality, ethical behavior, and proper interactions with the natural world *Jukurrpa*.[3] These are glimpses of how Indigenous Nations have matured a keen sense of reverence and responsibility for our relationship with Mother Earth. These insights can help our shared world develop a more sustainable relationship with Nature today.

Ecological belonging is the ultimate realization of being part of the collective Mother Earth system. It is the recognition of our place in life cycles. It manifests as an Earth-group identity through affective (compassionate), cognitive (acknowledging), motivational (volitional), ethical (responsible), and ecological (stewarding) engagement with life forms and phenomena in the natural world. It asserts one of the earliest insights I shared with you, that there is no human flourishing without Mother Earth flourishing *first*.

Ecological belonging can encourage powerful psychological and social benefits with its soothing yet activating effects. Most important, perhaps, is how reverence for Mother Earth orients our actions toward stewarding the Lands. While one may usually think of reverence within metaphysical concepts, it can be tangible. Our relational, embodied, emotional, and responsible relationship with Mother Earth contributes to the flourishing of the world around us. Practices of kin relationality and ecological belonging strengthen our symbiotic relationships, since flourishing depends on environmental flourishing. Relating to the world is an awakening during re-wilding experiences and immersion in natural spaces. For instance, instead of centering the benefits of the forest on humans, we center on how we can benefit the forests. We could think of forest-fostering instead of forest-bathing.

The relationship with the cycles of nature imbued in Indigenous sciences aligns with current research on flourishing. When living closer to nature, the immune system shows higher levels of antibodies and less adrenaline in the blood.[4] A more earthly orientation improves mental well-being, reduces animosity and melancholy, and dramatically boosts energy.[5] Humans who live in harmony with the natural world experience heightened parasympathetic activity in their nervous system, which fosters cooperation.[6] Better relationships with ourselves, other people, and the environment are the outcome of these experiences.

Consider the Chiapas and Guatemalan Maya health system. It is a sophisticated social practice that focuses on fostering positive relationships with the environment to maintain balance, cleansing antisocial and antienvironmental tendencies and nurturing connection. Their coordinated response to adaptation, threats, illness, and disease, as well as their final acceptance of and surrender to death, are all based on these tenets.

The Maya health system demonstrates reverence through symbolic narratives, social and cultural constructs, beliefs, practices, and the use of natural resources as medicines. A cosmogonic worldview establishes an ethics of care, which maintains equilibrium throughout the cosmos. Through participatory practices that foster a connection to Mother Nature, Maya science and spiritual medicine establish the basis of interdependence, complementarity, and balance. For example, the *K'oponej witz* (Mountain Priest) of the Tzeltal Maya of Chiapas is a Spirit medicine practitioner whose primary healing involves communicating with the mountains. They pray to the Spirit of Mother Earth and inquire about needed actions to recover a natural equilibrium. Western medicine has yet to include similar environmental health practices.

The Indigenous emphasis on belonging to a community calls to mind Nature's regenerative, nourishing quality. Indigenous identities are strongly associated with the Land and its food sources, as expressed in many Indigenous cosmogonies. The connection between lineage and nature manifests in the reverential bond that Indigenous Peoples have with their ancestors. Ancestors are honored in annual ritual celebrations that follow the solar and lunar calendrical systems linked to agricultural cycles. People invoked ancestors as guides in agricultural practices, hunting times, war strategies, healing, and initiation rituals.

About 80 percent of the world's remaining biodiversity is managed by Indigenous Peoples, amounting to nearly 35 percent of the remaining protected Territories. Traditionally, the forests that Indigenous Peoples steward through their management systems have been much better protected than others in Abya Yala.[7] According to the United Nations Food and Agriculture Organization (FAO), the United Nations Development Programme (UNDP), and the United Nations Environment Programme (UNEP), these areas have lower carbon footprints than non-Indigenous zones.[8] In addition, they have lower deforestation rates.[9]

The FAO's 2021 report *Forest Governance by Indigenous and Tribal Peoples* found that the forests of these Indigenous Territories are crucial to mitigating climate change and conserving biodiversity. The report warned that more significant investment and political support is required to efficiently protect these natural areas and the cultures of the Indigenous Peoples who protect and depend on them.

Recently, a robust Indigenous movement has arisen to establish councils for communal Land tenure.[10] These assemblies aim to promote ecological belonging through equity and access to Land and natural resource management and conservation benefits. In keeping with Indigenous wisdom on the collective health of living beings and ecosystems, they emphasize how access to clean energy, water, and food sovereignty can impact Indigenous and planetary health.

In 2017, the FAO, UNEP, World Organization for Animal Health (OIE), and the World Health Organization (WHO) welcomed an astonishingly similar attempt at planetary health called the One Health approach.[11] This interagency effort aims to achieve better public health outcomes by recognizing that the health of humans, domestic and wild animals, plants, and the wider environment (including ecosystems) are closely linked and interdependent. In other words, the One Health approach points to our need for ecological belonging.

A year later, in 2018, the Declaration of Astana affirmed the international commitment to the milestone aspiration by recommending that traditional medicine systems become a crucial part of global health systems.[12] Lastly, in July 2022, the United Nations General Assembly declared the universal right to a clean, healthy, and sustainable environment for everyone, closely followed by the 2022 Nature-Based Solutions Initiative.[13]

These initiatives reflect healthy cycles of production and reproduction in partnership with Mother Earth. They underscore that our continued well-being depends on the well-being of all life forms. The way to such a transformation is collaboration among our diverse ways of being, sensing, knowing, and acting. The practices of Indigenous contemplation we have begun to engage with through story, art, visualization, and movement are ways of conversing with a responsive world and realizing its nuanced language. They allow glimpses into a self-transcendent state of awareness, care, and safety for ecological belonging and coexistence and bonds of reciprocity between Mother Earth and human health. They reveal guidelines for community living and relating in a way that enhances everyone's collective rights to flourishing.

We partner with our surroundings through kin relationality, the body seed, the luminous experience of the senses and emotions, and their development into heartfelt narratives. Our experience relates to every phenomenon within the ecosystem. And it is through the ecosystem that we relate to and create ourselves, others, and Mother Earth.

Return of the Feathered Serpent

The symbol of the serpent is the embodiment of wisdom in numerous Indigenous and other world traditions. Mesoamerica has the Feathered Serpent *Quetzalcoatl*; the Maya, the Feathered Snake *K'uk'ulkan*; in West, Central, and Southern Africa, there is the deity Snake Mermaid *Mami*

Wata; Hinduism speaks of the Coiled Snake *Kundalini*; and Buddhist and Jain traditions have the serpent beings *Nāgas*, which gave way to the mythic Naga Peoples of ancient Sri Lanka.

The harmful reputation the serpent has gotten in Abrahamic traditions sharply contrasts with Indigenous cosmovisions.

My reading of the Feathered Serpent of the Nahua and Maya pantheons (*Quetzalcoatl* and *K'uk'ulkan*, respectively) is that it personifies the energy of potentialities—the opportunity to awaken to the transcendent awareness of awe, reverence, and love for all of existence. It is the solar deity symbolizing consciousness and spiritual realization.

The Winged or Feathered Serpent traverses imperceptible realms, bridging the experience of the subtle body, the unconscious, and the afterlife. Such a transition allows the promise of new life: rebirth, renewal, and reemergence.

Humans are most noticeably matter—senses, blood, and bones—brought to life by the fruits of Mother Earth and the early electric spark of Spirit. Distillation and purification occur through various steps along the unending journey from the chaos of self-centered arrogance to the order (cosmos) of self-transcendent service. The body is exposed (metaphorically) to extreme conditions: floods, wildfires, being evaporated into the wind, devoured by hungry ghouls, composted in the soil, and so on. The process eventually allows for a reemergence, creating a new life form. A renewed spirited matter sublimates a body *made of* Spirit by connecting it to the heart of Mother Earth and the cosmic Universe.

The Feathered Serpent speaks of that journey from chaos to order, from the Underworld to the forestland to the hidden waters and then to the Skies. It points to every human being's creative capacity to offer ourselves in service to Mother Earth, to whom we owe our lives. It is an everlasting spiral journey through birth, death, and renewal. It is a timeless dream, a collective effervescence, a ceremony, a shared experience of soul-making. We turn to ashes only to come back from our Ancestors' bones and the blood of the Divine. We come back to life transformed, reunited, and restored. It speaks of our continuing evolution and comprehension and our realization that there is no awakening unless there is a collective awakening. *Flourishing Kin* emphasizes the turns of the spiral of attention outward, inward, and through. All paths point to the realization of our ecological belonging.

We share experiences with the world. We flourish by participating in others' flourishing. By connecting, we embody community. Our kin relationality weaves our collective body seeds through the luminosity of our senshine experience. The insights of our heartfelt wisdom engender our sense of ecological belonging, manifesting in interrelated actions in the presence of and with others. In such an Earth community, we find solutions, and where there is no ultimate answer, we find the right questions to discover infinite adaptations of possibilities. Each holds pieces of a shared experience that enrich the wisdom of our community.

We enhance our learning from the possibilities the Serpent weaves into the realms of experience. We invoke the presence of Mother Earth consciousness through the Winged Wisdom in our daily lives. Through stewardship and conservation for collective flourishing, we practice our reverence and responsibility to our human and non-human kin.

Stewardship and Indigenous-Led Conservation

The Intergovernmental Panel on Climate Change (IPCC) warns that the unprecedented environmental crisis will continue to worsen in all regions of the planet with irreversible changes over the following centuries. These changes will intensify the adverse living conditions of vulnerable populations worldwide. Following the Paris Agreement, carbon neutrality targets and solutions are becoming competitive across power and transport sectors. However, the IPCC urges an even more direct, prompt, and large-scale reduction in greenhouse gas emissions and the immediate phase-out of fossil fuels to limit climate warming. Alongside legal structures, the international community must develop lines of work associated with designing and implementing innovative green economies and clean production processes to transform consumption lifestyles feasibly.

The crises are the climate and economic crises caused by capitalism; social crises caused by colonialism and coloniality, modern slavery, mass incarceration, white supremacy, patriarchy and heteronormativity; and mental health crises caused by hopelessness and despair. Deaths of despair are part of the public health and economic crisis that has provoked the most extended sustained decline in life expectancy in the United States since the 1990s, mainly due to substance abuse, suicide, and cardiovascular diseases.[14]

The latest report on the Sustainable Development Goals warned that as of May 2022 a quarter of the world is living under the threat of war, a record 100 million people have been forcibly displaced worldwide (41 percent are children), and the accelerated degradation of the environment is projected to cause a 40 percent increase in disasters by 2030, resulting in 700 million people displaced and 10 million hectares of forest lost to deforestation.[15]

Climate displacement forcibly removes Indigenous Peoples more than any other group from their Territories. Likewise, the pandemic impacted Indigenous communities much more than the rest of the world. Moreover, Land defenders in Indigenous communities lose their lives at a higher rate trying to stop the rapacious and insatiable extractive industries.[16] Mexico, my homeland, ranks fourth among the world's most dangerous countries for environmental and Indigenous rights defenders.[17] The Special Rapporteur on the Rights of Indigenous Peoples observed that Mexico does not adequately follow international standards of free, prior, and informed consent and that a shocking 99 percent of cases of human rights violations against Indigenous Peoples go unpunished, in particular those against extractive megaprojects and drug cartels.[18]

The 2030 Sustainable Development Agenda as a proposal for action for the stewardship of humanity and the planet—promoting human development, sustainability, and continuous inclusive growth based on human rights and the conservation of our planet—requires more Indigenous involvement in decision-making processes of international cooperation and governmental commitment to establish legally binding frameworks that defend the rights of Mother Earth. It seems far-reaching, especially after the decline in development indicators due to the COVID-19 pandemic. In addition, the climate crisis is intensifying inequity, insecurity, and social and environmental instability in the most vulnerable populations.

Around the globe, the most vulnerable among us—children and youth, women and girls, people with disabilities, migrants, refugees, Indigenous Peoples, LGBTIQ+ people, and the Elderly—are facing a growing gap of marginalization, structural discrimination, and political exclusion.[19] Their basic needs are largely unmet: access to safe housing, clean water, sanitation, and nutritious food. At the same time, they suffer constant stigmatization and criminalization in laws, policies, and practices.

The most susceptible regions also face the most significant obstacles to sustainable well-being: Sub-Saharan Africa, Latin America and the Caribbean, and Oceania (excluding Australia and New Zealand). These regions have a very high percentage of Indigenous Peoples, especially communities with small populations, those in voluntary isolation, or those in an initial contact process. Having disaggregated information in all these regions seems to be still impossible, making it difficult to determine the best lines of action.

As a regional grouping, Latin America and the Caribbean have the most significant inequality gap globally. While it is not the most impoverished region, the wealth gap provokes social insecurity and levels of violence more intense than any other region, which makes it challenging to establish equality, health, and development. Political instability in the region generates economic uncertainty and limits political participation. As a result, stewardship and conservation efforts do not reach these populations.

When developing local and global partnerships to promote collective flourishing, we must focus on the societies and ecosystems bearing the brunt of physical changes in the climate and the impact on the ecological health of humans and more-than-human communities. Based on community and collaboration, ecological belonging offers practical solutions for intercultural inclusion and dialogue on sustainable development.

Contemplation is the art of truth, flourishing a path of connection, reverence a source of action, and bliss a way of healing. Can these

Indigenous methods be the helpful considerations for collective well-being that we may need to become living organisms that belong?

Creating culturally aware legal frameworks that respect tradition is necessary to bridge the gap between disciplines and organizational development models. These advantages result from spiritual reverence for Mother Earth, the creation of socially beneficial community structures, and the moral goal of coexisting peacefully with the environment.

Humans can change individualistic and egocentric views by building more connected, inclusive, diverse communities, institutions, and societies that value social awareness and cooperative behavior. Examples of these include the contemplative approach and international development agendas.

Spirit Flourishing

Cosmovisions frame the interpretation that Spirit is the source of the universe. Spirit is the fundamental force that keeps the universe spinning and serves as the animating principle of life in an endless web. Spirit is the source of the world's order. Spirit is family. Spirit is relating kin.

The spiritual path points to the realization of possibilities. The only way to live it is by internalizing our part in the ecosystem and embracing the constantly changing balance and flow. The concept of health and well-being does not only refer to the absence of disease, confusion, or delusion. It demands reciprocity to the world, a personal relationship and responsibility to the Lands and all other beings. It requires that we be stewards of our environment and one another. The possibility of collective flourishing lives on this path of truth, connection, reverence, and bliss.

The crises has forced a deep global reflection on the meaning of well-being and the practices to cultivate and sustain it. We are at a critical moment in rejecting the limitations of the established colonial, exclusive, and individualistic perspective and creating a new path forward aimed at collective flourishing. This urgent challenge requires reflection on diverse solutions focused on collective rights and sustainability.

Contemplative studies advance this discourse by stimulating awareness of social-emotional-ethical-spiritual learning and living.

Contemplation is Truth, Flourishing is Connection, Reverence is Action, and Bliss is Healing epitomize the Indigenous collective approach to well-being. These elements support resilience in terms of sustainable development in line with appropriate relationships with Indigenous Peoples by fostering cooperation, restoration, and risk mitigation. A shared commitment to intergenerational community processes that support education, health, safety, and land and territory protection, as well as the provision of reparations and advances in technology, is necessary. These processes should be based on both traditional and modern technologies.

The astounding diversity of Indigenous Peoples reveals unique identities, territorial relationships, customs, institutions, legal frameworks, and traditional knowledge. Despite this diversity, there is consensus regarding our sense of ecological belonging and our acute duty to take care of and show reverence for the ecosystem. One commonality amongst the diversity of Indigenous cultures is the belief that the Land bestows life—human health originates from a healthy environment.

One more time: there is no human flourishing without Mother Earth flourishing.

Indigenous stewardship and the conservation of ecosystems go hand in hand with the reclamation of governance and autonomy over traditional territories, natural resources, and cultures. Capacity-building and innovation are models of conservation through clean energy sources. However, the prevailing legacies of colonialism and coloniality continue to undermine environmental health significantly, keeping Lands and Peoples at never-before-seen risks of biocultural extinction.

Self-determination, protection from discrimination, autonomy in community affairs, development, political engagement, access to federal funds, rights to Lands, territories, and resources, governance, and recognition are all included in the list of Indigenous rights. Based on the complementarity, plurality, and multidimensionality of our cosmovisions and the pillars of kin relationality and ecological belonging, these rights orient to the Indigenous perspective of self-determined well-being.

However, these rights have yet to receive true legal recognition to be considered a global reality.

Only two of the 232 indicators of global development progress are related explicitly to Indigenous concerns. One of the major social factors contributing to a decline in our standard of living, for instance, is limited access to health care. Therefore, as cultural bridges between health systems and community values, the international community should incorporate intercultural perspectives of health and well-being into policies, programs, and reproductive health services.[20]

Nevertheless, the extraordinary resilience of Indigenous Peoples has allowed an advance in sustainable collective well-being rooted in traditions and customs. This system is based on the recovery of practices focused on land management, Indigenous-led conservation, and community building and support. Of particular importance in ongoing efforts are the revitalization of traditional languages, political participation, and the protection of natural resources against the erosion and eradication of the biodiversity produced by climate change.

Research shows a strong correlation between linguistic loss, the climate crisis, and biodiversity loss in the tropical belt.[21] Since the world loses an Indigenous language every two weeks, and with it a whole worldview, the right to autonomy, self-determination, and free, prior, and informed consent to all matters of Indigenous traditional systems, medicines, and cultures is a vital component of biocultural conservation.[22] The benefit sharing and responsible management of resources, including reparations for the use of any tangible and intangible heritage of Indigenous systems, is inextricably linked to the restoration and conservation of Mother Earth.

Until recently, Indigenous voices were absent from the strategic planning, policymaking, and decisions to alleviate the environmental constraints that damage ecological conservation. Indigenous participation in planetary health approaches promotes governance of Lands and Territories, the commons as shared resources for conservation and stewardship, respect for the feminine, respect for the Lands, intercultural health for humans and the environment, and a developed practice of ethical and spiritual living that elicits kindness, generosity, reverence, and a sense of awe, love, and sacredness for life.

At the United Nations Biodiversity Conference in December 2022, more than 190 countries (of a total of 194) signed the 30x30 historical global biodiversity framework.[23] This landmark agreement provides a strategic vision and a global roadmap for the conservation, protection, restoration, and sustainable management of biodiversity and ecosystems to preserve biodiversity in the planet's 30 percent of lands and waters by 2030. Such a commitment acknowledges the urgency of policy action worldwide and locally to stabilize biodiversity loss by 2030. If carried out rightfully, it may allow for the recovery of Mother Earth by 2050. However, as was previously said in chapter 3, good intentions can lead to fatalities, and some of contemporary history's most horrific land-grabbing incidents have taken place in the name of conservation. To make room for multinational corporations involved in clean energy, Indigenous Peoples have been brutally forced from their Lands in Africa, Asia, and Abya Yala.

Indigenous knowledge of our ecological place, of Nature as a nurturing mother and caregiver, and of our role in the intricate web of relationships that makes up the Mother Earth system is becoming more and more apparent. More and more people are realizing that protecting Mother Earth's health comes first for human health.

PRACTICE

Ecological Belonging

This practice encourages reflections on the Lands and the shared crisis emergencies calling for ecological belonging to our shared natural world. It inspires action to give voice to human and more-than-human voices so that we can learn about them from them. By investigating the ways of the lineages of Lands and Ancestors, we learn to listen to the language of Mother Earth and realize that we are warped and weft and wed in life with all living beings and phenomena, our blood- and earth-lines. The practice fosters an understanding of our place and future.

Like seedlings to the Sun are the subtleties of interactions, the tenderness of interactors, and the fragility of interbeing, all looking for the light of nourishment and the warmth of connection. These unique aspects of presence coalesce in the roots of the moment, shaped by belonging and togetherness.

We honor those Earth warriors of the heart who have been uprooted from home yet keep offering themselves for collective well-being.

We engage with these stories and orient toward the transformative possibility of belonging to our ecological system to flourish kin.

The first part of this practice encourages you to delve into the present conversation with the meaning of belonging. In the second part, following the dialogue with your perceptions allows you to explore the intuitive aspects of an interactive experience with the systems of life around you.

Don't anticipate a single outcome.

Permit yourself to feel how the practice affects and changes you.

Turn off your devices or put them elsewhere if you haven't done so already.

Locate a spot where you are comfortable.

Make the location you've chosen accessible. Ideally, your practice should be available daily, anywhere at any time.

No matter where you are, pay attention to how your emotions manifest and change.

Allow your muscles to relax in a manner that guarantees your focus and ease.

The path should be gradual, gentle, and soothing yet encourage us to move little by little beyond our comfort zone.

Pause

We take in the subtle surroundings by settling into our bodies,
keeping our eyes open,

we gently focus as we follow the texture of emerging relationships.
We follow the light of attention,
revealing connections in the surrounding natural world.

Let's come to a new venture embracing wholeness.
We sense our being and body,
becoming breath, heart, mind, memories, and imagination
moving beyond our single story, our single seed,
we grow into a collective grove.

Center in your breath.
From your breath, turn to your heart.
Then go into the silent secret of your heartbeat,
And further into the deep-rooted mystery of the heartbeat of the Earth
almost imperceptible.

Sense it to find it.

Our natural being is an extensive, responsive system.
In and around you.

Mother Earth's heart.

Beating in waves of experience.
Open,
it carries you in a gentle,
rhythmic,
constant
sway.

It is the river of belonging,
flowing through soils and quenching thirsts
of hearts and hopes.

It surrounds the sack of early seeds of home
sources of community.

Within this shared heart-beating seeds settle in presence.

Welcome what is
your perfectly imperfect perception
No right, no wrong, no way.
Only the way of flow.

Raw space

Expanding—contracting

The heartbeat is the welcoming of Mother Earth.

Her soft, warm embrace, softly being.

Being and belonging
Being and beating
Being and sharing
with the seeding of Mothers

From the depths to the breath
to belonging, being, and becoming.

Open

Welcoming wholeness:
the warm brightness and the moist coolness:
Earth and Skies—Soil and Sun
in your heart.

Mother Earth humming
her calling
her heartbeat throbbing.

Her one voice
guiding fear to safety,
anger to action,
grief to meaning,
despair to transformation.

Bridges open when our beings
—whole—
Open.

Trust emerging
Life
She ripples
She hums
pulses
quivers

She sighs
murmurs
under the Skies.

In the Quest for Insight

As a reminder, this practice takes the path of experience and inner visu-alization. You attempt an intimate sensing experience of the beating of the world to sense the living essence of the planet. Perhaps this experi-ence gives you a more intimate, novel, and sensorial way to belong and embrace others from a perceived shared existence.

The practice is an entry point for the meaning of belonging through a sensory experience and interactive connection. The relationship with the Earth through your heartbeat and the planet's is expansive and most subtle to your present.

In the following part of the practice, in this quest for meaning, you are invited to inquire into this experience and how it may provoke action for caring for the larger community of living beings.

The following cues further this reflection and elicit insight into your relationship with the planet.

Let these cues animate your experience.

Feel each of them as they rise in the body, heart, mind, memory, imagination, and belonging.

Let them simmer.

Let what connects you to the world emerge.

Continue your pursuit of understanding beyond introspection, taking part in learning from the Lands themselves with the people who live in them, both human and non-human. Approach those who inhabit this planet with you and start a conversation in the way that other practices in this book have led you to do. Carry on the discussion on how we create our belonging, and move toward becoming an ecological human.

- How does the practice encourage accountability for our part in the present emergency?

- How do we reflect in a constructive way that builds bridges rather than burning them down?

- How does it look for you to develop a responsible relationship with the Lands by learning about them?

- Write some notes in your cherished journal-chest.

To listen to this practice, follow the link yuriacelidwen.com or the QR code on the table of contents.

12

Reparations Through
Right Relationships

Said the tongue of my forebears
in the navel part of Abya Yala
that long ago—so far back that time was not yet born
when the world was just begot
the gods came together to make those to roam on Earth.

They wanted beings of Spirit, beings of flow.
Yet, easier said than done,
as you and I know,
only practice leads to progress,
even for the gods.

And so, for each attempt, a sun became:
the sun of Earth,
the sun of Wind,
the sun of Fire,
and sun Sol of Water.

Every time the gods failed miserably.
The creatures turned out rigid and uptight,
arrogant and full of deceit.
So, the gods sent chaos to these creatures:
jaguars to devour them,
gusts of wind to blow them away,
fires to scorch and blaze them,
and floods to dilute and drown them.

And yet, the gods gave up not.

Decided, they tried one last time
and made our current sun:
the Sol of Movement,
who keeps all things warm
and changing in constant flux.

The solar god Quetzalcoatl, the Feathered Serpent,
descended to the Mictlan, the land of the dead.
He went to bring the precious bones of previous eras,
the seeds from which—hopefully—
a new kind of being would emerge.

Arriving before the Lord of the Dead, he said:
"I have come for the bones you safeguard.
We need them to sprout new beings of Spirit."
And so replied Mictlantecutli:
"You will have the bones only after you play the sacred conch
and walk four times around the seat of precious stones."

The shell, however, had no holes.
Quetzalcoatl called on the brother worms
to make the holes, and so they did.
Without delay, the gentle sister bees flew in
and buzzed within their most mellifluous chant.

When you listen carefully
deep within your heart,
you may still feel the bee's vibration
coming from their song
deep within the heart of the earth.

Mesmerized by the sound,
Mictlantecutli gave the bones;
but once out of the trance,
he wanted them back!
Trick after trick, he tried to retrieve them
but time and again, the Feathered Serpent recovered them.

Finally, leaving the Mictlan,
Quetzalcoatl ascended to the Tamoanchan,
the place of the eternal life
and gave the bones to the Greatest Mother Goddess
Quilatzi Cihuacoatl Tlazolteotl
the Warriorress Snake Goddess
of Purification and Renewal.

She threw the seed bones in her earth womb
and kindly and lovingly ground the bones to ashes.
The Feathered Serpent bled his lightning rod on the ashes
and together with Mother Goddess
churned blood and ashes into human form.

The new creatures were hungry
but there was nothing for them to eat.
Sister red ant told of the sacred maize
hidden in the caves of the earth.
Turned into a black ant, Quetzalcoatl
together with red ant brought the maize,
the gods chewed on it to make a paste
and placed it on our lips.

So, we came to life

OUR HUMAN COMMUNITIES have been dislocated and used as weapons against each other. How can we compost the continuous, internalized coloniality from systems that humiliate, erase, and disregard our traditions and knowledge? Ancestral knowledge teaches that we can become food for others through harmonious relationships with environmental communities. What are these skillful pathways?

For millennia, Indigenous traditional medicine systems have gathered extraordinary wisdom on the healing properties of natural beings for wounds of the soul and the soil. More than only addressing disease and distress, these medicines are aimed at gathering spiritual meaning, balance, and belonging. Indigenous Peoples on all continents learned through observation and experience about these medicines' properties, benefits, interactions with other remedies, dosages, and side effects. To this day, three-quarters of the population in the Global South continues to use and rely on traditional medicine from plants, fungi, animals, microorganisms, and mineral sources.[1] For thousands of years, they depended on their traditional systems for health and happiness. That is, before Western medicine began to exploit this tangible and intangible Indigenous heritage by isolating and synthesizing ingredients and developing drugs that would be administered in pill form and expected to have rapid results that would require very little orientation or integration. To grow medicine and health care into booming economic industries.

Pharmacognosy (medicine knowledge and the development of drugs from natural sources) has extracted most of its discoveries from the traditional systems preserved by Indigenous Peoples. To this day, even in the Global North, almost half of the drugs in the United States are derived from the traditional use of natural ingredients, and a quarter of all prescription drugs contain at least one natural source ingredient.[2]

Yet traditional systems remain dismissed as ineffectual or superstitious, relegated as inferior to Western medicine. In some regions of the world, practitioners are denigrated, persecuted, criminalized, and threatened. Indigenous traditional doctors are painfully underpaid, follow the same trends as their people for lower life expectancies, and lack the resources to practice their healing traditions effectively. In other words, Western medicine has appropriated, capitalized, and commodified Indigenous knowledge for its sole health and economic benefit.

In recent years, no other medicine research has attracted as much interest and investment as that of Spirit medicines, or what the West calls psychedelics. The hype has taken over pharmaceutical and medical research and public interest, with estimates of 50 million US users propagating a burgeoning multibillion-dollar industry. This fast-growing field is severely concerning for Indigenous Peoples with long-standing traditional use of Spirit medicines. If history has anything to tell us, this trend threatens to damage their traditions and Lands irreversibly.

Indigenous traditional healers feel a solid commitment to participating in social justice struggles because these extractions are wounding Mother Earth. Agricultural multinationals poison the soils with pesticides, fungicides, and herbicides that erode the Lands, as if the West had declared war against Nature. If She is sick, no medicine grows. There is no life; there is no humanity. We know that if She hurts, so do humans. The diseases of the body and the mind—supremacy, individualism, greed, discrimination, loneliness, isolation, and so on—result from a total disconnect from spirituality. Lack of harmony results in more disease and increased desperation to find solutions that are harder to find.

Indigenous Elders have warned that medicines are hiding away deeper into less disturbed areas. Alarming changes are happening due to the climate emergency. Rising temperatures affect the life cycles and health of plants, fungi, animals, and minerals, resulting in too-variable-to-predict times for harvesting. Climate burdens are not the only problem. Finding medicine, even for traditional local use, has become more challenging due to overharvesting for tourist demands. Spiritual consumerism, environmental degradation and deforestation, monocropping, traditional transformation adopting imported medicines, and local conflicts between communities competing for funding to cater to Western demands are excruciating challenges that Indigenous traditions increasingly face.

The most challenging of these concerns is the clashing of ways of being. Indigenous traditions consider the use of Spirit medicines as sacred. The sacred cannot be negotiated or commercialized. Its approach is ceremonial wisdom to learn aspects of our spiritual relationship and responsibility to our planet. The medicines open spiritual gateways to our past and emerging Ancestors of blood and Lands. They dissolve the obstacles of the narrow human mind that has lost its ability to be in community and promote an experience of transcendence through kin relationality and ecological belonging to Nature, the Universe, and Spirit.

Indigenous traditions regard these medicines as revealers of the animating principle of life, Spirit. In contrast, Western approaches regard the human mind as a singular atomic entity. The term *psychedelics*—coined by Humphrey Osmond in 1957—suggests they can manifest the mind or reveal its beneficial properties. The term strips the medicines from their spiritual aspect, reducing them to servants of the human mind alone.

In the West, the medicalized, self-development, and recreational use of psychedelics focuses on the benefits to the individual—from mental health disorders targeting treatment-resistant depression, anxiety, post-traumatic stress disorder (PTSD), and addictions to achieving the highest human potential or creativity to recreational use at festivals or for individual use. Using classic psychedelics—such as ayahuasca, psilocybe mushrooms, and peyote—has also spawned markets, from psychedelic churches to festivals and underground therapies in which Western facilitators charge thousands of dollars per service.

How do we overcome the communication divisions between such different worldviews and different Peoples?

Ethical Applications of Indigenous Wisdom

Mutually beneficial relationships can only happen through cultivating repair. Acknowledging when there have been violations and committing to reparations can ensure a path toward reciprocal, respectful, and culturally informed systems.

After many years of research and activist work regarding the stark realities of Western extraction, exploitation, capitalization, and commercialization of our tangible and intangible heritage, it became evident to me that the detriment to Indigenous Peoples, traditions, and our environments needs justice. I centered on properly recognizing Indigenous traditions as the origin of Spirit medicine, educating research institutions to commit to ethical practices and sharing benefits with Indigenous communities. I sought ways to support traditional medicine by establishing lines of reparation and beneficial relationships between Indigenous and Western medicine systems based on international frameworks protecting Indigenous rights. Above all, I demanded the representation of Indigenous voices in developing Western psychedelic research to restore the authority of Indigenous goals, methodologies, and approaches to Spirit medicines and to benefit all communities involved, as is aligned with our traditions of collective well-being.

I realized it was crucial to amplify the voices of the traditions that the Western appropriation of Spirit medicines has impacted the most. In desperate search of justice and solutions, I convened a group of Indigenous traditional medicine practitioners, activists, Tribal lawyers, and scholars from around the world to discuss skillful actions and joint initiatives decided by consensus and to counteract Western predatory practices.

While still federally criminalized in the United States, many states are preparing legislation to make psychedelic medicine widely available. This growing availability is alarming since no international framework refers explicitly to protecting and regulating Indigenous traditional medicine to ensure its ethical use at the local, regional, and international levels.

With very different influences and stages of development, some frameworks have explored the access and regulation of herbal medicine, but none regarding Spirit medicines. Among those that mention herbal medicine are Decision 391 on the Common Regime on Access to Genetic Resources of the Andean Community (CAN) and its modifications in Decisions 423, 448, the International Conference of Drug Regulatory Authority (ICDRA), the Pan American Network for Drug Harmonization and Regulation (PANDRH), and the International Conference on Harmonization of

Technical Requirements for Pharmaceutical Products for Human Use (ICH). These documents are discussions between regulatory authorities and the pharmaceutical industry on scientific and technical aspects of pharmaceutical products to develop guidelines for use and regulation in the pharmaceutical sector. None discuss the participation of Indigenous Peoples nor respect our rights to free, prior, and informed consultation regarding access to our tangible heritage of herbal medicine.

The Convention on Biological Diversity and its Protocol of Nagoya and the Declaration of Sharms are the only international agreements that promote and safeguard the fair and equitable sharing of the benefits derived from the use of Indigenous genetic resources. The Protocol provides a solid foundation for greater legal certainty and transparency for both providers and users of resources. The provisions of the Protocol regarding access to traditional knowledge of Indigenous and local communities, when such knowledge is related to genetic resources, strengthen our communities' capacity to benefit from using their knowledge, innovations, and practices. However, not all countries are signatories of this Convention. The United States is not a signatory and is unlikely to become one in the near future.

With this in mind, the group I convened created a manifesto to protest the current state of psychedelic research and to propose solutions for rightful relations with Indigenous Peoples. This consolidated document, entitled "Ethical Principles of Indigenous Traditional Medicine to Guide Western Psychedelic Research and Praxis" was published in *The Lancet Regional Health: Americas* on December 16, 2022.[3] This article presented eight ethical guidelines that explore pathways of reparations to Indigenous traditions for the violations of our heritage.

In this chapter, I have expanded these guidelines to ten principles that may serve to establish right and respectful relationships with Indigenous wisdom traditions that lead to collective flourishing.

TEN ETHICAL PRINCIPLES FOR COLLECTIVE FLOURISHING[4]

Acknowledgment	Reverence Respect
Education	Reckoning Responsibility
Reparations	Regulation Reparation
Belonging	Restoration Renovation
Reemergence	Reciprocity Reemergence

For a world of flourishing kin, there is no other way onward than to have a rooted self-identity of ecological belonging. Such a view restores dignity by establishing relationships based on Ethical Principles for collective flourishing: (1) reverence, (2) respect, (3) reckoning, (4) responsibility, (5) regulation, (6) reparation, (7) restoration, (8) renovation, (9) reciprocity, and (10) reemergence.[5]

1. Reverence

The worldviews of Indigenous Peoples are cosmogonic; that is, they come from or originate from the cosmos or universal wisdom. Mother Earth is the vision and explanation of the world of life. Therefore, our practices are values that relate to and explain life in terms of the relationships within living systems. These worldviews lay the foundations for kin relationality. They foster the unity and harmonic balance necessary for developing spiritual and material life. Indigenous spiritualities transcend the dogmatic views of reductionist, essentializing perspectives. Many Indigenous practices integrate the physical with the subtle.

Indigenous traditional medicine is a system of holistic balance through ethical values that interrelate humans and the environment in the form of temporal interrelatedness known as spiral time. This system is based on reverence for all life forms and a commitment to preserve them. It prompts insights into compassionate living and an awareness of collective care, with each action impacting the sustenance and well-being of future generations. Reverence for Mother Earth, Her Peoples, and all phenomena is our key to collective well-being.

2. Respect

A respectful approach to Indigenous ways of being, thinking, and doing requires interacting with Indigenous knowledge systems through authorized traditional knowledge holders within specific contexts. This includes not only respectfully following protocols but also receiving authorization to use and modify Indigenous knowledge in new contexts.

3. Reckoning

Reckoning with the perpetuation of colonialism and coloniality against Indigenous cultures involves fierce scrutiny and examination of Western practices of domination, extraction, and appropriation of Indigenous heritage. The West must not only acknowledge but also be held accountable for these ongoing destructive practices and for the white-supremacist legacies in research systems and education.

4. Responsibility

The erasure and exclusion of Indigenous sciences by research institutions was used to justify genocidal practices and our systemic oppression. The scientific and academic communities must address their participation in imperialist, capitalist, and white-supremacist education systems that exclude non-Western religious traditions, philosophies, and ways of knowing. If academic institutions can acknowledge these failures, hold themselves accountable, and practice diversifying and decolonizing their approach toward research and education, Indigenous communities can begin building a bridge toward ethical and sovereign weaving in of Indigenous Knowledge systems. Research institutions can strive toward genuine relevance by weaving in Indigenous Knowledge systems, with the participation of Indigenous Peoples. We look for a commitment to removing barriers to equitable and inclusive education access. We create spaces of relevance to communities by incorporating Indigenous traditions through local, communal, historical, and sacred understandings of cultural practices and traditional worldviews, espousing concern in promoting Indigenous self-determination and sovereignty.

5. Regulation

We call for the creation of a strict legal mechanism for intellectual property that recognizes the right of Indigenous Peoples to their intangible inheritance and provides them with the benefits derived from the use and development of medicines and practices of Indigenous origin—particularly those that were extracted and appropriated without their free, prior, and direct informed consent. Returning the benefits to the communities of origin requires a direct commitment to the established rights of Indigenous Peoples.

6. Reparation

Reparation systems are required to promote and safeguard Indigenous self-determination: the practice and revitalization of cultural and spiritual traditions and customs; the maintenance and development of past, present, and future manifestations of cultures; the repair and restitution of appropriate cultural, intellectual, religious, and spiritual property without free, prior, and informed consent; the right to maintain, control, protect and develop cultural heritage, traditional knowledge, and manifestations of science, technology and culture; the recognition and protection of social, cultural, religious, and spiritual values and practices; the fair and equitable sharing of benefits derived from the use of genetic resources, as well as proper cross-border cooperation and increased awareness, capacity building, and technology transfer, collaboration, and cooperation; the use, administration, and conservation of natural resources and community health services that are under the responsibility and control of Indigenous Peoples; and the guarantee of intercultural education at all levels.

7. Restoration

Restoring places of authority in the decision-making processes that impact Indigenous Peoples in the ethical guidelines of research fields and of the institutional review boards (IRB) demonstrates a direct commitment to reparations and involvement and collaboration led by Indigenous practitioners through free, prior, and informed consent (FPIC) and within the cultural protocols of the communities. This collaboration will be dictated by the rights of intellectual property, data science, and knowledge sovereignty that establish the position of Indigenous Peoples on the ethical use of traditional medicine and the main focus on relationships between humans and more-than human-beings, the non-commercial use of ancestral medicine, and these ten ethical principles focused on the well-being of the planetary community.

8. Renovation

Indigenous traditional knowledge systems should involve local, national, and international cooperation with governmental and non-governmental organizations and humanitarian and environmental bodies to establish restorative and transitional and transformative justice procedures to highlight Indigenous discourse and promote capacities rooted in Indigenous ontologies (ways of being). We call for an Indigenous body in the form of a review board or council that ensures that these ten ethical principles are enacted across research, training programs, facilitators, and so on.

9. Reciprocity

Reciprocity exists in relationships of equality. Extreme power differentials impede reciprocity with Indigenous people disproportionately suffering from military, political, and economic forces, globalized tendencies, and practices of extraction. Paths to reciprocity must be preceded by transitional and restorative justice where safe spaces and equal access to influence and decision-making are possible.

10. Reemerging

The initial cycle of *Flourishing Kin* along the spiral path of collective well-being is reemerging. The enduring tale of our capacity for contemplation keeps returning to the observation, embodiment, storytelling, and reflection of shared experience. It serves as a reminder that although challenges will inevitably arise, the slow route proceeds in a spiral. This pattern sums up life as ever-evolving and cyclical. It is reminiscent of continuous progress that keeps returning home to a familiar place, yet never meeting on the same grounds. It is an homage to our continuous transformation and reemergence.

This last principle requires a pause and a turn to a new cycle of the spiral path. We move to a new beginning, a new story.

The next chapter is a culmination and invitation to a new cycle. We dive deeper into this crucial principle of reemerging. Please consider it a more extended contemplation into truth, flourishing, reverencing, and healing through bliss.

PRACTICE

Seedlings of the Earth

As we reflect on right relationships, let's return to the ways of my Maya lineage, calling on the *Metik K'inal*, las Abuelitas de la Tierra, the Grandmothers of the Earth, who embody the true right relationships with all our Sibling beings: truth, connection, reverence, and bliss. With this remembrance comes *Metik Xmucané*, the matron of midwives and newborns and the Grandmother of the Maya Divine Twins in the Popol Vuh, the creation story we have been visiting along with *Flourishing Kin*. Metik Xmucané reminds us of opportunities in the unexpected as she plants and tends to seedlings on the Earth.

Let yourself be free to explore how the practice moves and transforms you. Do not expect one specific result.

If you haven't done so, turn off your devices or leave them in a different place.

Find a place where you feel comfortable and observe how your surroundings manifest.

Make your chosen place easy to access. Your practice should ideally be accessible at any time and place in your daily life.

Let your body rest in a way that helps you to stay relaxed but attentive.

The path should be gradual, gentle, and soothing yet encourage us to move little by little beyond our comfort zone.

Pause

Hunahpú and Ixbalanqué, the Maya Divine Twins,
are embarking on their Underworld journey
to face a duel with the Lords of Xibalbá,
Lords of Death,
who want to erase humanity from Mother Earth.

The Divine Twins, concerned but hopeful, say to Metik Xmucané,
Our Grandmother of the Earth:
"Metik, please plant these seeds in the forest garden.
If they dry up, you will know we have perished.
But if they rise,
you will know we are returning
safe and sound
to life."

Concerned and frightened, not knowing what will come,
Metik Xmucané goes to her Mother's Garden.

The Sun is out and burning.
His anger is hot.
He rises with no sign of ease.
She fears her children's fate.
Distressed, she cries.
Disturbed and troubled for her children, she cries.
She cries and cries her sorrow and her pain.

She had no idea that her tears were soothing.
Calming, healing, and quenching thirst.
They were the waters the seeds needed
to become conscious and rise.

Tiny little seedlings sprout
at Metik Xmucané's surprise! And she rejoices
at the seedlings sprouting in her home!

Caring for the soul of the world
For each of her saplings
Past, present, and those yet to come
Singing her song
and reemerging

Reemerging

THE NATURAL FIRST Law established by Spirit, Our Creator and Shaper of life, confirms that everything has saplings. We request the blessing of Metik Xmucané to be the truth, connection, reverence, and bliss to guide us in the opportunity of regeneration. We all can become food for others. May we be nourished to give life to the next cycle of the heart.

These narratives are how Indigenous Peoples have related to and made sense of our presence and purpose.

We own our part in the mess that has become our presence on Mother Earth. We become accountable, reflective, and humble to our kin.

We dig into the mud to let the crack open wide. We welcome the watering flows of early Spring showers and let the hidden petrichor from the core of the rock.

We pay attention, and all we hear is urgency.
Our challenges are innumerable,
but also infinite are our opportunities.
Our grief is daunting,
but also heartening is our compassion.
Stories are organic because they are created;
they can be composted and regenerated.

In these pages, I have invited you into the bridging and weaving of hearts: from yours to others and then back to the very heart of Mother Earth. Our spiral path started gradually with connection and community as a vessel for sustainable collective well-being. Now, we return to Mother Earth to renew our commitment to raising her narratives.

Mother Earth *claims us*.

We become the seed of a new shared story interwoven with intention and care. This web of care and concern for Mother Earth commits all beings and phenomena in a path of spiritual becoming, of honoring Spirit, the animating principle of life.

We complete our first cycle around the spiral path and return with lessons learned, practices tried, and insights gained. Now we reemerge on the path, moving on and gradually advancing as we engage with new questions about planetary flourishing.

One last time, let me insist:
There is no human flourishing
without Mother Earth flourishing first.

These pages have attempted to give rise to action pathways to reciprocate Mother Earth for the generous, abundant, vibrant diversity of life. We continue to walk toward collective flourishing, embracing more lessons, practices, and insights into the power of community and connection. It is a spiral path bridging Indigenous and Western sciences for a promise of a caring world.

This historic moment encourages us to make sense of our suffering and reflect on new stories of collective transformation toward reverence and bliss centered on flourishing kin through collective well-being. We see the shadow in the eye of the harm caused by generations of human othering of self, others, and Mother Earth. And so we aspire to a heartful reckoning with our past and flourishing collaboration and partnerships for restorative solutions that benefit Mother Earth. We aspire to transform our identities from self-centered individuals to flourishing kin, to emerge from the acorn to the grove.

We look for the opportunity for regeneration—the reemergence of a collective story grounded in the Indigenous foundations for collective well-being: of kin relationality and Mother Earth reverence; of the body seed that contains communities; of the luminous potentiality of the senses to bring experience to full awareness; of the heartful wisdom of colorful, loving plurality; and the spiritual becoming turning othering to ecological belonging.

The bridges of Indigenous ancestral wisdom with Western compassion, science, and kindness provide the seeds of care and a roadmap toward cultivating a contemplative culture of truth, connection, reverence, and bliss. This is how we all flourish. This is the path of flourishing kin.

Reemerging

K'uxtaya!

K'uxtaya! k'uxtaya! k'uxtaya!
te sjocholil kuxinele, yu'un te lajele, te cha'tojkele.
Ya sk'uxtabe sjocholil te sak'inale
sok te ijk'al Lumilale.

Ya sk'uxtabe sp'ijil te Ch'ulme'tike!
sok ya sk'uxtabe ak'ol k'inal yu'un te Ch'ultatike!

k'alal k'anuk ta nakomalil te kuxinele,
bit'il tulan talelil te nojem nax ta ijk'al xab
peta nax aba te ta ch'ultesbil kuxinele
te xlemlun nax stilel ta sjamlejal te awo'tane

Translation from Tzeltal:

Love!

Love! Love! Love!
the emptiness of being, of death, of birth
love the emptiness of clarity
and of the thickest mud.

Love the lunar wisdom!
Love the solar joy!

And when the inklings of life
appear hard and harsh and full of rifts
rejoice in the ecstatic bliss
that burns in the openness of our becoming

Let us transit to the beginningless times of the spiral with a story.
It will be a familiar story.

It will be a story of blame, shame, self-loathing, and condemnation of "the other" that morphs into remembrance, resilience, reverence, and love.

Once upon the greenery of my years, panic held me in his grip of uncertainty. I was barely hanging from the horns of the moon with no safety net underneath. Mere existence hurt in beauty and dismay, bliss and horror. Not unlike today.

Stories run fast about a world inert, dreamless, merely for stock . . .

Domination bolsters loss—subjugation furthers bondage.

These tales of alienation and division, conquest and defeat—they paralyze us. Unable to act, we become sterile, fearing our creativity due to our destructive power over the world.

What wicked influence convinced us
of guarding an inner cell
against our dreams?

Roaming in the maze of powerlessness, unable to belong, I had little of the sweetness of youth and was heavy in the bitter taste. I was too young for wisdom and already too exhausted from fighting for my life. Between recklessness and hopelessness, I dared the world to counter back.

Time felt rock rigid then. Lithic. Inescapable from my own rigidity of unattainable control.

I was yet to learn that uncertainty *is* freedom.

I imagined humanity carrying a heart of stone. Then, I realized Elder rocks are made of tiny sibling particles—slowly, slowly packed together. While they may seem as if weighed down by time, most often buried, silent, and left for dead, they are still porous. Channels between the Siblings run, through which water and wind flow. There is a song resounding in their heart.

Their hearts are full of reverence, their wisdom full of Spirit from the Lands.

And so, this was their song:

Dear One, we know very well the mud you're in.
Know its breadth.
Surrender.
Still.
In its depth lays the acorn's dream of groves.
Your story, while it seems your own,
is always woven with others.
Now, a thread looking for warp and weft;
later, a web of food shared,
a good home to all others.

Theirs is a gift of trust, a gift of commitment. These words are water that does not resist but coheres. These words bridge time, the past into the future, spiraling into this present moment when you read them. These are the stories of my Elders that return sowing seeds of reverence, of home, of love. It is a love that weaves in collective ways. A love that reaches your heart, warping and wefting into a colorful fabric of plurality.

Loving the world
it opens and flows
reemerging

Glossary

aesthetic arrest: First used by James Joyce in *A Portrait of the Artist as a Young Man*, the expression *aesthetic arrest* is used in *Flourishing Kin* to describe the transcendence that unfolds in the direct experience of beauty. A dissolution of self-identity or self-arrest follows the moment of sublimation, as if in the experience of spiritual presence, we are held in both stillness and perpetual movement.

Ajq-ijab: Maya "keepers of time" who are considered spiritual guides and traditional medicine practitioners.

animic entities: These are essences of subtle energy that stir to action or give life to the dispositions or temperaments of a person. They set in motion and motivate behavior. The influence of these entities can encourage a sense of balance, well-being, and flourishing.

body seed: One of the Indigenous foundations for well-being. Just as a seed carries all material for the plant to flourish and bear fruit, the body can be seen as a seed of possibilities that can engender actions for the benefit of the larger community of beings in service to Mother Earth.

chrysopoeia: The alchemical process of turning lead into gold, it is a metaphor for spiritual awakening or for turning the base. It is the transformation from unconscious reactivity into spiritual consciousness, with a profound awareness of relationality that benefits the greater good.

cosmovisions: A synonym for worldviews. Cosmovisions are outlooks about the world that attempt to make meaning of the interactions and relationships occurring among living beings and phenomena in all their contextual configurations.

ecological belonging: This Indigenous principle for well-being conceptualizes the self as belonging to a kin-relational, collective Earth system network that includes its ecosystems and life cycles. It manifests as a recognition of belonging to a planetary identity. It orients us toward benefiting life forms and the natural world through affect (compassion toward living forms), cognition (recognition and acknowledgment of the interdependence of living forms), volition (intention and responsibility for the Earth as a network of beings and phenomena), and motivation (stewardship for the thriving of that community of beings and phenomena). In ecological belonging, all of existence belongs to environmental systems and networks.

heartfelt wisdom: This Indigenous principle for well-being describes the composting of self-centered perceptions and the regeneration of compassion and care practices for humans *and* more-than-human beings.

kin relationality: This Indigenous principle for well-being refers to the Indigenous relationship-based way of being, in which living beings and phenomena are recognized as part of a family lineage. In such conceptions, each being and phenomenon shares a familial bond of group identity and of interdependence, mutuality, and organization. In kin relationality all of existence is deemed a Relative.

Metik: Mother in Maya Tzeltal.

Metik K'inal: Mother of the Earth.

naguales: These are energetic influences that rule and orient behavior in accordance with astronomical observations during contemplative practice. They are twenty in the Maya calendar and in the Nahua Mexica calendar.

Pison Q'Ajq'al: Medicine practitioners and "keepers of time" called *Ajq-ijab* carry a medicine bag or sacred wrapping that, among other things, contains seeds that signify the cosmological cycles of the sacred Maya calendar.

senshine: A playful coming together of *senses* and *sunshine* to look at how we use all of our senses to brighten our experience of life. Involving the heart, imagination, memory, reason, sound, sight, touch, smell, and taste, senshine nurtures the observation of direct experience as a source of traditional knowledges.

tonalpohualli: From Nahuatl *tonal* + *pōhualli*, meaning "to give light count," also understood as the count of days in the Nahua Mexica 260-day sacred calendar composed of a *veintena* (twenty) of *trecenas* (13-day) periods.

trecena: A noun determining a group of thirteen objects. The noun is used frequently in calendric systems in Mesoamerica.

tsampa: Toasted barley flour that is a food staple in Tibet.

veintena: A noun determining a group of twenty objects that is used frequently in calendric systems in Mesoamerica.

xiuhpōhualli: From Nahuatl *xihuitl* + *pōhualli, meaning* "year count." This was the solar 360-day + 5 silent days in the Nahua Mexica calendar. The calendar was composed of 18 twenty-day months and five days of silence or reflection considered inauspicious; thus, these five days were days of atonement.

Xmucané: The Grandmother of the Divine Twins in the Maya creation story Popol Vuh. She is also the matron of midwives and newborn children. It has been suggested that the name Xmucané may mean "She who plants a seed in the Earth."[1]

xukulen: Ceremonial cosmological observations that follow the calendric system of the Maya Peoples.

Notes

Introduction

1. Jonathan Loh and David Harmon, *Biocultural Diversity: Threatened Species, Endangered Languages* (Zeist, The Netherlands: World Wildlife Fund, 2014), wwfint.awsassets.panda.org/downloads/biocultural_report __june_2014.pdf.

2. Joseph Henrich, *The WEIRDest People in the World: How the West Became Psychologically Peculiar and Particularly Prosperous* (New York: Farrar, Straus and Giroux, 2020).

3. Evan Thompson, *Why I Am Not a Buddhist* (New Haven, CT: Yale University Press, 2022).

4. John Welwood, "Principles of Inner Work: Psychological and Spiritual," *Journal of Transpersonal Psychology* 16, no. 1 (1984): 63–73, atpweb.org /jtparchive/trps-16-84-01-063.pdf; Yuria Celidwen et al., "Ethical Principles of Traditional Indigenous Medicine to Guide Western Psychedelic Research and Practice," *The Lancet Regional Health: Americas* (February 2023), doi.org/10.1016/j.lana.2022.100410.

5. Marie Battiste, "Cognitive Imperialism," in *Encyclopedia of Educational Philosophy and Theory* (Springer, 2018): 183–188, doi.org/10.1007/978-981 -287-588-4_501; Harold Roth, "Against Cognitive Imperialism: A Call for a Non-Ethnocentric Approach to Cognitive Science and Religious Studies," *Religion East and West* 8 (October 2008): 1–26.

Some Critical Notes

1. INALI, Náhuatl, Instituto Nacional de Lenguas Indígenas, inali.gob.mx /clin-inali/html/l_nahuatl.html.

2. Federico Navarrete, "The Path from Aztlan to Mexico: On Visual Narration in Mesoamerican Codices," *Res: Anthropology and Aesthetics 37* (Spring 2000): 31–48, doi.org/10.1086/RESv37n1ms20167492.

3. "Linguistic Maps of Mesoamerica," FAMSI: Foundation for the Advancement of Mesoamerican Studies, famsi.org/maps/linguistic.htm.

4. A. C. Ramírez, and M. del C. "Nahuatl in numbers," Dirección de Lingüística del Instituo Nacional de Antropología e Historia, 2020, linguistica.inah.gob.mx/index.php/leng/92-nahuatl.

5. "Health," United Nations Department of Economic and Social Affairs: Indigenous Peoples, un.org/development/desa/indigenouspeoples /mandated-areas1/health.html.

6. "10 Things to Know about Indigenous Peoples," United Nations Development Program, July 29, 2021, stories.undp.org/10-things-we -all-should-know-about-indigenous-people; Nicole Redvers, Yuria Celidwen et al., "The Determinants of Planetary Health: An Indigenous Consensus Perspective," *The Lancet Planetary Health* 6, no. 2 (February 2022): e156–e163, doi.org/10.1016/S2542-5196(21)00354-5.

7. Claudia Sobrevila, *The Role of Indigenous Peoples in Biodiversity Conservation: The Natural But Often Forgotten Partner* (Washington, DC: The International Bank for Reconstruction and Development/The World Bank, 2008), documents.worldbank.org/curated/en/995271468177530126/The -role-of-indigenous-peoples-in-biodiversity-conservation-the-natural-but -often-forgotten-partners; Stephen T. Garnett et al., "A Spatial Overview of the Global Importance of Indigenous Lands for Conservation," *Nature Sustainability* 1 (July 2018), doi.org/10.1038/s41893-018-0100-6.

8. Á Santamaría, *Redes transnacionales y emergencia de la diplomacia indígena: Un estudio a partir del caso colombiano*, Universidad del Rosario (2008).

Chapter 3: Flourishing as Connection

1. *The Sustainable Development Goals Report 2022*, United Nations, unstats.un.org /sdgs/report/2022/The-Sustainable-Development-Goals-Report-2022.pdf.

2. "Joint Tripartite (FAO, OIE, WHO) and UNEP Statement Tripartite and UNEP Support OHHLEP's Definition of 'One Health,'" United Nations Food and Agriculture Organization (FAO), World Organisation for Animal Health (OIE), World Health Organization (WHO), United Nations Environment Programme (UNEP), wedocs.unep.org/bitstream /handle/20.500.11822/37600/JTFOWU.pdf.

3. Angola Andorra et al., "The Human Right to a Clean, Healthy and Sustainable Environment," United Nations, July 26, 2022, digitallibrary .un.org/record/3982508.

4. "Environmental Impacts of Wind Power," Union of Concerned Scientists, March 5, 2013, ucsusa.org/resources/environmental-impacts -wind-power.

5. Dan Brockington, Rosaleen Duffy, and Jim Igoe. 2010. *Nature Unbound: Conservation, Capitalism and the Future of Protected Areas*. Reprinted. London: Earthscan. Igoe, Jim. 2021. *The Nature of the Spectacle On Images, Money, and Conserving Capitalism*. s.l.: University of Arizona Press. Igoe, Jim. 2022. "5 National Parks and Human Ecosystems The Challenge to Community Conservation. A Case Study from Simanjiro, Tanzania." *In Conservation and Mobile Indigenous Peoples*, edited by Dawn Chatty and Marcus Colchester, 77–96. Berghahn Books. doi.org /10.1515/9781782381853-009.

6. Victoria Burnett, "Mexico's Wind Farms Brought Prosperity, But Not for Everyone," *New York Times*, July 26, 2016, nytimes.com/2016 /07/27/world/americas/mexicos-wind-farms-brought-prosperity-but -not-for-everyone.html; A. K. Delgado, "The Struggles of the Wind in Tehuantepec," *El País*, July 18, 2016; elpais.com/elpais/2016/07/15 /planeta_futuro/1468592019_398642.html.

7. *Forest Governance by Indigenous and Tribal Peoples: An Opportunity for Climate Action in Latin America and the Caribbean*, Food and Agriculture Organization of the United Nations, 2021, doi.org/10.4060/cb2953en.

8. Antoine Lutz, John D. Dunne, and Richard J. Davidson, "Meditation and the Neuroscience of Consciousness: An Introduction," in *The Cambridge*

Handbook of Consciousness, ed. Philip David Zelazo, Morris Moscovitch, and Evan Thompson (Cambridge: Cambridge University Press, 2007).

9. Perle Besserman, *The Shambhala Guide to Kabbalah and Jewish Mysticism* (Boston: Shambhala, 1997).

10. Thomas Merton, *Contemplative Prayer*, Introduction by Thich Nhat Hanh (New York: Image, 1971).

11. *Encyclopedia of Islam*, 2nd ed. (The Netherlands: Brill, 2012); Oludamini Ogunnaike, *Poetry in Praise of Prophetic Perfection: A Study of West African Arabic Madī Poetry and Its Precedents* (Cambridge: Islamic Texts Society, 2020).

12. Gilles Polian, *Diccionario multidialectal del tseltal: tseltal-español* (México, D.F. Instituto Nacional de Lenguas Indígenas, 2018).

13. Marc Thouvenot, Javier Manríquez, and Miguel León-Portilla, *Diccionario náhuatl-español: basado en los diccionarios de Alonso de Molina con el náhuatl normalizado y el español modernizado*, primera edición (México, D.F.: Universidad Nacional Autónoma de México Fedeicomiso Felipe Teixidor y Monserrat Alfau de Teixidor, 2014).

Part 2: Reverencing

1. Martinez Cobo. 1981. "Martínez Cobo Study | United Nations for Indigenous Peoples." E/CN.4/Sub.2/476. United Nations. un.org/development/desa /indigenouspeoples/publications/2014/09/martinez-cobo-study/.

2. José Martínez Cobo, *Martínez Cobo Study*; "Alta Outcome Document," Global Indigenous Preparatory Conference for the United Nations High Level Plenary Meeting of the General Assembly, to be known as the World Conference on Indigenous Peoples, June 2013, unorg/esa/socdev /unpfii/documents/wc/AdoptedAlta_outcomedoc_EN.pdf.

3. United Nations Declaration on the Rights of Indigenous Peoples, 2007, un.org/esa/socdev/unpfii/documents/wc/AdoptedAlta _outcomedoc_EN.pdf; Matt Wildcat and Daniel Voth, "Indigenous

Relationality: Definitions and Methods," *AlterNative: An International Journal of Indigenous Peoples* 19, no. 2 (May 2023): 475–483, doi: 10.1177/11771801231168380.

Chapter 4: Indigenous Peoples and Reverence in Action

1. C107—Indigenous and Tribal Populations Convention, 1957 (No. 107), International Labour Organization, ilo.org/dyn/normlex/en/f?p =NORMLEXPUB:12100:0::NO::P12100_ILO_CODE:C107; C169— Indigenous and Tribal Peoples Convention, 1989 (No. 169), International Labour Organization, ilo.org/dyn/normlex/en/f?p=NORMLEXPUB: 12100:0::NO::P12100_ILO_CODE:C169.

2. Martinez Cobo. 1981. "Martínez Cobo Study | United Nations for Indigenous Peoples." E/CN.4/Sub.2/476. United Nations. un.org /development/desa/indigenouspeoples/publications/2014/09/martinez -cobo-study/.

3. United Nations Declaration on the Rights of Indigenous Peoples, 2007, un.org/development/desa/indigenouspeoples/wp-content/uploads/sites /19/2018/11/UNDRIP_E_web.pdf.

4. "Alta Outcome Document," Global Indigenous Preparatory Conference for the United Nations High Level Plenary Meeting of the General Assembly, to be known as the World Conference on Indigenous Peoples, June 2013, un.org/esa/socdev/unpfii/documents/wc/AdoptedAlta _outcomedoc_EN.pdf.

5. "10 Things to Know About Indigenous Peoples," United Nations Development Program, July 29, 2021, stories.undp.org/10-things-we-all -should-know-about-indigenous-people.

6. *The Indigenous World 2022*, ed. Dwayne Mamo, International Work Group for Indigenous Affairs, iwgia.org/en/documents-and-publications /documents/indigenous-world/english/603-iwgia-book-the-indigenous -world-2022-eng/file.html; "SDG Indicators: Regional Groupings Used in Report and Statistical Annex." Retrieved June 26, 2024, from United

Nations Sustainable Development Goals, unstats.un.org/sdgs/indicators
/regional-groups.

7. "China," International Work Group for Indigenous Affairs, iwgia.org
    /en/china; "The Indigenous World 2022: Myanmar," International Work
    Group for Indigenous Affairs, iwgia.org/en/myanmar/4654-iw-2022
    -myanmar.html.

8. National Bureau of Statistics, stats.gov.cn/tjsj/ndsj/2021/indexch.htm.

9. "Uyghur Tribunal Judgment," as delivered at Church House,
    Westminster, December 9, 2021, uyghurtribunal.com/wp-content
    /uploads/2021/12/Uyghur-Tribunal-Summary-Judgment-9th-Dec-21.pdf.

10. "The Industries Causing the Climate Crisis and Attacks Against
    Defenders [Annual]," Global Witness, en/campaigns/environmental
    -activists/last-line-defence/ ; "2020, In Numbers: Lethal Attacks Against
    Defenders Since 2012," Global Witness. Retrieved June 1, 2022, from
    en/campaigns/environmental-activists/numbers-lethal-attacks-against
    -defenders-2012/.

11. J. Daniel Oliva Martínez, *Diversidad, resistencia y utopía: Los pueblos
    indígenas de nuestro tiempo* (Valencia: España: Tirant Humanidades, 2022).

12. "Transforming Our World: The 2030 Agenda for Sustainable
    Development," United Nations Department of Economics and
    Social Affairs: Sustainable Development, September 2015, sdgs.un.org
    /2030agenda; United Nations Declaration on the Rights of Indigenous
    Peoples, 2007, un.org/development/desa/indigenouspeoples/wp-content
    /uploads/sites/19/2018/11/UNDRIP_E_web.pdf; C169—Indigenous
    and Tribal Peoples Convention, 1989 (No. 169), International Labour
    Organization, ilo.org/dyn/normlex/en/f?p=NORMLEXPUB:12100:0::
    NO::P12100_ILO_CODE:C169; "What is the IACHR?" Inter-American
    Commission on Human Rights IACHR, oas.org/en/IACHR/jsForm/
    ?File=/en/iachr/mandate/what.asp; Text of the Convention on Biological
    Diversity, Convention on Biological Diversity, cbd.int/convention/text;
    Inter-American Commission on Human Rights, oas.org/en/IACHR
    /jsForm/?File=/en/iachr/mandate/what.asp; "International Covenant on

Civil and Political Rights," United Nations Human Rights: Office of
the High Commissioner, December 16, 1966, ohchr.org/en/instruments
-mechanisms/instruments/international-covenant-civil-and-political-rights.

13. Grace Jaramillo, "Latin America: Trade and Culture at a Crossroads,
International Journal of Cultural Policy 25, no. 5 (July 2019): 602–614, doi
.org/10.1080/10286632.2019.1626847.

14. Zoha Shawoo and Thomas F. Thornton, "The UN Local Communities
and Indigenous Peoples' Platform: A Traditional Ecological Knowledge-
Based Evaluation," *WIREs Climate Change* 10, no. 3 (February 2019), doi
.org/10.1002/wcc.575.

15. Gregory A, Cajete, "Indigenous Science, Climate Change, and
Indigenous Community Building: A Framework of Foundational
Perspectives for Indigenous Community Resilience and Revitalization,"
Sustainability 12, no. 22 (November 2020), mdpi.com/893136.

16. "IWGIA Annual Report 2020," International Work Group for
Indigenous Affairs, June, 2021, iwgia.org/en/resources/publications/305
-books/4416-ar2020.html; "'Spectre of Poverty' Hangs Over Tribes and
Indigenous Groups: UN Labour Agency," UN News, February 3, 2020,
news.un.org/en/story/2020/02/1056612.

17. "Health," United Nations Department of Economic and Social Affairs:
Indigenous Peoples, un.org/development/desa/indigenouspeoples
/mandated-areas1/health.html.

18. "Non-Discrimination: Groups in Vulnerable Situations," United
Nations Human Rights: Office of the High Commissioner, ohchr.org
/EN/Issues/Health/Pages/GroupsInVulnerableSituations.aspx.

Chapter 5: Epistemological Equity by Elevating Indigenous Sciences

1. *The 11th Hour*, written by Nadia Conners, Leila Conners Petersen, and
Leonardo DiCaprio, Warner Independent Pictures, 2008.

2. Joseph Henrich, *The WEIRDest People in the World: How the West Became Psychologically Peculiar and Particularly Prosperous* (New York: Farrar, Straus and Giroux, 2020).

3. Angayuqaq Oscar Kawagley, Delena Norris-Tull, and Roger A. Norris-Tull, "The Indigenous Worldview of Yupiaq Culture: Its Scientific Nature and Relevance to the Practice and Teaching of Science," *Journal of Research in Science Teaching* 35, no. 2 (February 1998): 133–44, doi.org/10.1002/ (SICI)1098-2736(199802)35:2<133::AID-TEA4>3.0.CO;2-T.

4. Nicole Redvers, Yuria Celidwen, Clinton Schultz, Ojistoh Horn, Cicilia Githaiga, Melissa Vera, Marlikka Perdrisat, et al. 2022. "The Determinants of Planetary Health: An Indigenous Consensus Perspective." *The Lancet Planetary Health* 6 (2): e156–63. doi.org/10.1016 /S2542-5196(21)00354-5.

5. López Austin, *Cuerpo humano e ideología: Las concepciones de los antiguos nahuas* (Universidad Nacional Autónoma de México: Instituto de Investigaciones Antropológicas, 1984).

6. Alison Gerlach, "Thinking and Researching Relationally: Enacting Decolonizing Methodologies with an Indigenous Early Childhood Program in Canada," *International Journal of Qualitative Methods* 17, no. 1 (May 2018), doi.org/10.1177/1609406918776075.

7. Marlene Castellano, "Updating Aboriginal Traditions of Knowledge," in *Indigenous Knowledges in Global Contexts,* edited by George Dei, Budd L. Hall, and Dorothy Goldin Rosenberg (Toronto: University of Toronto Press, 2000); Judy Iseke, "'Indigenous Storytelling as Research'" *International Review of Qualitative Research* 6, no. 4 (2013): 559–77; J. Iseke, and B. Brennus, "Learning Life Lessons from Indigenous Storytelling with Tom McCallum," in *Indigenous Philosophies and Critical Education: A Reader*, edited by George J. Sefa Dei, 245–61 (New York: Peter Lang, 2011); M. Kovach, *Indigenous Methodologies: Characteristics, Conversations, and Contexts.* (Toronto: University of Toronto Press, 2009); S. Wilson, *Research Is Ceremony: Indigenous Research Methods* (Black Point, NS: Fernwood Publishing, 2008).

8. Eve Tuck and Marcia McKenzie, "Relational Validity and the 'Where' of Inquiry: Place and Land in Qualitative Research," *Qualitative Inquiry* 21, no. 7 (March 2015): 633–638, doi.org/10.1177/1077800414563809.

9. Emma Elliott-Groves, Dawn Hardison-Stevens, and Jessica Ullrich, "Indigenous Relationality Is the Heartbeat of Indigenous Existence During COVID-19," *Journal of Indigenous Social Development* 9, no. 3 (November 2020): 1–3.

10. Monica Gratani et al., "Indigenous Environmental Values as Human Values," *Cogent Social Sciences* 2, no. 1 (May 2016), doi.org/10.1080 /23311886.2016.1185811.

11. "Alta Outcome Document," Global Indigenous Preparatory Conference for the United Nations High Level Plenary Meeting of the General Assembly to be known as the World Conference on Indigenous Peoples, June 2013, un.org/esa/socdev/unpfii/documents/wc/AdoptedAlta _outcomedoc_EN.pdf.

12. Nicole Redvers et al., "Indigenous Natural and First Law in Planetary Health," *Challenges* 11, no. 2 (2020), doi.org/10.3390/challe11020029; Yuria Celidwen, "Indigenous Contemplative Science: An Ethics of Belonging and Reconnection," The Center for Contemplative Mind in Society, May 29, 2020, YouTube video, youtube.com/watch?v= nJNNKLeB57g; Monica Gratani et al., "Indigenous Environmental Values as Human Values," *Cogent Social Sciences* 2, no. 1 (2016), doi.org /10.1080/23311886.2016.1185811.

13. Victor Hugo Torres Dávila, *La acción pública intercultural: Las políticas interculturales de los gobiernos indígenas* (Ecuador: Universidad Politécnica Salesiana et al., 2009), dspace.ups.edu.ec/bitstream /123456789/6173/1/La%20accion%20publica%20intercultural.pdf; FAO and FILAC, Forest Governance by Indigenous and Tribal People: An Opportunity for Climate Action in Latin America and the Caribbean (FAO, 2021), doi.org/10.4060/cb2953en; Nicole Redvers, Yuria Celidwen, Clinton Schultz, Ojistoh Horn, Cicilia Githaiga, Melissa Vera, Marlikka Perdrisat, et al. 2022. "The Determinants of Planetary Health: An

Indigenous Consensus Perspective." *The Lancet Planetary Health* 6 (2): e156–63. doi.org/10.1016/S2542-5196(21)00354-5.

14. Jean M. Twenge, W. Keith Campbell, and Elise C. Freeman, "Generational Differences in Young Adults' Life Goals, Concern for Others, and Civic Orientation, 1966–2009," *Journal of Personality and Social Psychology* 102, no. 5 (2012): 1045–1062, doi.org/10.1037/a0027408.

15. Birgit Koopmann-Holm and Jeanne L. Tsai, "The Cultural Shaping of Compassion," in *The Oxford Handbook of Compassion Science*, edited by E. M. Seppälä et al. (New York: Oxford University Press, 2017): 273–285.

16. Jennifer E. Stellar et al., "Class and Compassion: Socioeconomic Factors Predict Responses to Suffering," *Emotion* 12, no. 3 (June 2012), doi: 10.1037/a0026508.

17. Sarah D. Pressman, Brooke N. Jenkins, and Judith T. Moskowitz, "Positive Affect and Health: What Do We Know and Where Next Should We Go?" *Annual Review of Psychology* 70 (January 2019): 627–650, doi.org/10.1146/annurev-psych-010418-102955.

Chapter 6: Intergenerational Trauma and Intergenerational Bliss

1. M. Asante, "Foreword," in *Anti-Colonialism and Education: The Politics of Resistance*, ed. G. J. Sefa Dei and A. Kempf (Rotterdam: Sense Publishers, 2006).

2. Carl G. Jung, *Collected Works of C. G. Jung, Volume 9 (Part 2), Aion: Researches into the Phenomenology of the Self* (Princeton, NJ: Princeton University Press: 1969).

3. Giorgio Agamben, *Homo Sacer: Sovereign Power and Bare Life* (Stanford, CA: Stanford University Press: 1998).

4. Ernest Barker, Aristotle, and R. F. Stalley, *Politics* (New York: Oxford University Press, 2009).

5. Pope Alexander VI (1431–1503), "Demarcation Bull Granting Spain Possession of Lands Discovered by Columbus," Gilder Lehrman Collection, gilderlehrman.org/collection/glc04093.

6. John Leddy Phelan, *The Millennial Kingdom of the Franciscans in the New World* (Berkeley: University of California Press: 1970).

7. Maria Yellow Horse Brave Heart, "Gender Differences in the Historical Trauma Response Among the Lakota," *Journal of Health & Social Policy* 10, no. 4 (1999): 1–21, doi.org/10.1300/J045v10n04_01; Maria Yellow Horse Brave Heart, "The Historical Trauma Response Among Natives and Its Relationship with Substance Abuse: A Lakota Illustration," *Journal of Psychoactive Drugs* 35, no. 1 (2003): 7–13, doi.org/10.1080/02791072.2003.10399988; Sergio Flores-Hernández et al., "The Indigenous Condition in Health Services: Comparison of Quality in Care 2012–2018 for the Population in Poverty," *Salud Pública de México* 61, no. 6 (Nov–Dec 2019), doi.org/10.21149/10562.

8. *Front Line Defenders Global Analysis 2021*, Front Line Defenders, February 23, 2022, frontlinedefenders.org/en/resource-publication/global-analysis-2021.

9. "Health," United Nations Department of Economic and Social Affairs: Indigenous Peoples, un.org/development/desa/indigenouspeoples/mandated-areas1/health.html.

10. Cindy L. Ehlers et al., "Measuring Historical Trauma in an American Indian Community Sample: Contributions of Substance Dependence, Affective Disorder, Conduct Disorder and PTSD," *Drug and Alcohol Dependence* 133, no. 1 (November 2013): 180–187, doi.org/10.1016/j.drugalcdep.2013.05.011.

11. "Health," United Nations Department of Economic and Social Affairs: Indigenous Peoples.

12. Ryan K. Masters, Laudan Y. Aron, and Steven H. Woolf, "Changes in Life Expectancy Between 2019 and 2021 in the United States and 21 Peer Countries," *medRxiv* (April 2022), doi.org/10.1101/2022.04.05.22273393.

13. "What Is the Impact of COVID-19 for Indigenous Peoples' Rights?" United Nations Human Rights: Office of the Hig Commisioner, June 29, 2020, ohchr.org/Documents/Issues/IPeoples/OHCHRGuidance_COVID19 _IndigenouspeoplesRights.pdf; "Impact of the COVID-19 Virus on Indigenous Populations/Communities in Africa," press release from African Commission on Human and Peoples' Rights, 2020, achpr.au.int/en.

14. Maria Yellow Horse Brave Heart, "Gender Differences in the Historical Trauma Response Among the Lakota"; Maria Yellow Horse Brave Heart, "The Historical Trauma Response Among Natives and Its Relationship with Substance Abuse: A Lakota Illustration."

15. "Facts and Figures: Ending Violence Against Women," UN Women, unwomen.org/en/what-we-do/ending-violence-against-women/facts -and-figures.

16. *Women, Business and the Law 2016: Getting to Equal* (World Bank Group, 2015), efaidnbmnnnibpcajpcglclefindmkaj/pubdocs.worldbank.org/en /810421519921949813/Women-Business-and-the-Law-2016.pdf.

17. "Female Genital Mutilation/Cutting: A Global Concern," UNICEF, 2016, data.unicef.org/resources/female-genital-mutilationcutting-global-concern.

18. *The Sustainable Development Goals Report 2022*, United Nations, unstats.un .org/sdgs/report/2022/The-Sustainable-Development-Goals-Report-2022.pdf.

19. *Indigenous Peoples, Poverty and Human Development in Latin America*, ed. Gillette Hall and Harry Anthony Patrinos (London: Palgrave Macmillan, 2006), doi.org/10.1057/9780230377226.

20. *Mairin Iwanka Raya: Indigenous Women Stand against Violence*, International Indigenous Women's Forum (FIMI: 2006), fimi-iiwf.org /en/biblioteca-propias/mairin-iwanka-raya-indigenous-women-stand -against-violence.

21. Andre B. Rosay, "Violence Against American Indian and Alaska Native Women and Men: 2010 Findings from the National Intimate Partner and

Sexual Violence Survey (NISVS)," Interuniversity Consortium for Political and Social Research, June 9, 2016, doi.org/10.3886/ICPSR36140.V1.

22. "CDC Works to Prevent Violence Against American Indian and Alaska Native People Fact Sheet," Center for Disease Control and Prevention, cdc.gov/injury/pdfs/tribal/Violence-Against-Native-Peoples-Fact-Sheet.pdf.

23. "Missing and Murdered Indigenous Women and Girls: A Snapshot of Data from 71 Urban Cities in the United States," Urban Indian Health Institute, Seattle Indian Health Board, November 2018, uihi.org/wp-content/uploads/2018/11/Missing-and-Murdered-Indigenous-Women-and-Girls-Report.pdf.

24. "A Proclamation on Missing and Murdered Indigenous Persons Awareness Day, 2021," Joseph R. Biden, whitehouse.gov/briefing-room/presidential-actions/2021/05/04/a-proclamation-on-missing-and-murdered-indigenous-persons-awareness-day-2021.

25. "Exposure," UNDP Ecosystems & Biodiversity—ICCA. Retrieved December 18, 2022, from undp-biodiversity.exposure.co/categories/icca.

Chapter 7: Kin Relationality

1. Damiano Azzalini, Ignacio Rebollo, and Catherine Tallon-Baudry, "Visceral Signals Shape Brain Dynamics and Cognition," *Trends in Cognitive Sciences* 23, no. 6 (June 2019): 488–509, doi.org/10.1016/j.tics.2019.03.007; Antonio Damasio, *Self Comes to Mind: Constructing the Conscious Brain* (New York: Pantheon Books, 2010); Anil K. Seth and Manos Tsakiris, "Being a Beast Machine: The Somatic Basis of Selfhood," *Trends in Cognitive Sciences* 22, no. 11 (November 2018): 969–981, doi.org/10.1016/j.tics.2018.08.008.

2. Stephen W. Porges, "Polyvagal Theory: A Science of Safety," *Frontiers in Integrative Neuroscience* 16 (May 2022), doi.org/10.3389/fnint.2022.871227.

3. Michael Gurven et al., "From the Womb to the Tomb: The Role of Transfers in Shaping the Evolved Human Life History," *Experimental Gerontology* 47, no. 10 (October 2012): 807–813, doi.org/10.1016/j.exger.2012.05.006.

4. M. J. Hertenstein et al., "Touch Communicates Distinct Emotions," *Emotion* 6, no. 3 (2006): 528–533, doi.org/10.1037/1528-3542.6.3.528; Naomi I. Eisenberger, "Social Ties and Health: A Social Neuroscience Perspective," *Current Opinion in Neurobiology* 23, no. 3 (June 2013): 407–413, doi.org/10.1016/j.conb.2013.01.006.

5. Ming Kuo, "How Might Contact with Nature Promote Human Health? Promising Mechanisms and a Possible Central Pathway," *Frontiers in Psychology* 6 (August 2015), doi.org/10.3389/fpsyg.2015.01093.

6. Chia-Pin Yu et al., "Effects of Short Forest Bathing Program on Autonomic Nervous System Activity and Mood States in Middle-Aged and Elderly Individuals," *International Journal of Environmental Research and Public Health* 14, no. 8 (August 2017): 897, doi.org/10.3390 /ijerph14080897; J. Lee et al., "Effect of Forest Bathing on Physiological and Psychological Responses in Young Japanese Male Subjects," *Public Health* 125, no. 2 (February 2011): 93–100, doi.org/10.1016/j.puhe.2010 .09.005; Quing Li, "Effect of Forest Bathing Trips on Human Immune Function," *Environmental Health and Preventive Medicine* 15, no. 1 (March 2009): 9–17, doi.org/10.1007/s12199-008-0068-3.

7. Chia-Pin Yu et al., "Effects of Short Forest Bathing Program on Autonomic Nervous System Activity and Mood States in Middle-Aged and Elderly Individuals."

8. Quing Li, "Effect of Forest Bathing Trips on Human Immune Function."

9. Margaret M. Hansen, Reo Jones, and Kirsten Tocchini, "Shinrin-Yoku (Forest Bathing) and Nature Therapy: A State-of-the-Art Review," *International Journal of Environmental Research and Public Health* 14, no. 8 (July 2017): 851, doi.org/10.3390/ijerph14080851.

10. Julianne Holt-Lunstad, Timothy B. Smith, and J. Bradley Layton, "Social Relationships and Mortality Risk: A Meta-analytic Review," *PLoS Medicine* 7, no. 7 (July 2010), doi.org/10.1371/journal.pmed.1000316.

11. Dacher Keltner and Jonathan Haidt, "Approaching Awe, a Moral, Spiritual, and Aesthetic Emotion," *Cognition and Emotion* 17, no. 2

(2003): 297–314, doi.org/10.1080/02699930302297; Y. Bai et al. "Awe, the Diminished Self, and Collective Engagement: Universals and Cultural Variations in the Small Self," *Journal of Personality and Social Psychology* 113, no. 2 (2017): 185–209, doi.org/10.1037/pspa0000087.

Chapter 8: Body Seed

1. Joseph W. Bastien, "Qollahuaya-Andean Body Concepts: A Topographical-Hydraulic Model of Physiology," *American Anthropologist* 87, no. 3 (September 1985): 595–611, doi.org/10.1525/aa.1985.87.3.02a00050.

2. Mihaly Csikszentmihalyi, *Flow and the Foundations of Positive Psychology: The Collected Works of Mihaly Csikszentmihalyi* (New York: Springer, 2014).

3. Alan S. Cowen and Dacher Keltner, "Self-Report Captures 27 Distinct Categories of Emotion Bridged by Continuous Gradients," *Proceedings of the National Academy of Sciences* 114, no. 38 (September 2017): E7900–E7909, doi.org/10.1073/pnas.1702247114.

4. James N. Kirby et al., "The Current and Future Role of Heart Rate Variability for Assessing and Training Compassion," *Frontiers in Public Health* 5 (March 2017), frontiersin.org/articles/10.3389/fpubh.2017.00040.

5. Kohki Arimitsu and Stefan G. Hofmann, "Effects of Compassionate Thinking on Negative Emotions," *Cognition and Emotion* 3, no. 1 (2015): 160–167, doi.org/10.1080/02699931.2015.1078292.

6. J. L. Goetz, D. Keltner, and E. Simon-Thomas, "Compassion: An Evolutionary Analysis and Empirical Review," *Psychological Bulletin* 136, no. 3 (2010): 351–374, doi.org/10.1037/a0018807.

7. David Wallace Adams, *Education for Extinction: American Indians and the Boarding School Experience, 1875-1928* (Lawrence: University Press of Kansas, 1995.

8. John T. Cacioppo and William Patrick, *Loneliness: Human Nature and the Need for Social Connection* (New York: W. W. Norton & Co., 2009); Eric D. Wesselmann et al., "When Do We Ostracize?" *Social*

Psychological and Personality Science 4, no. 1 (April 2012): 108–115, doi.org /10.1177/1948550612443386.

9. Joseph P. Gone, "Redressing First Nations Historical Trauma: Theorizing Mechanisms for Indigenous Culture as Mental Health Treatment," *Transcultural Psychiatry* 50, no. 5 (2013): 683–706, doi.org/10.1177 /1363461513487669.

10. Paul Gilbert, *Compassion: Conceptualisations, Research and Use in Psychotherapy* (New York: Routledge, 2005).

11. Felix Warneken and Michael Tomasello, "The Roots of Human Altruism," *British Journal of Psychology* 100, no. 3 (May 2009): 455–471, doi.org/10.1348/000712608X379061.

Chapter 9: Senshine

1. Alfredo López Austin, *Cuerpo humano e ideología: las concepciones de los antiguos nahuas* (México: Universidad Nacional Autónoma de México, Instituto de Investigaciones Antropológicas, 1984).

2. Marc Thouvenot, Javier Manríquez, and Miguel León-Portilla, *Diccionario náhuatl-español: basado en los diccionarios de Alonso de Molina con el náhuatl normalizado y el español modernizado*, primera edición (Ciudad de México: Universidad Nacional Autónoma de México Fedeicomiso Felipe Teixidor y Monserrat Alfau de Teixidor, 2014).

3. Anik Debrot et al., "Is Touch in Romantic Relationships Universally Beneficial for Psychological Well-Being? The Role of Attachment Avoidance," *Personality and Social Psychology Bulletin* 47, no. 10 (2021): 1495–1509, doi.org/10.1177/0146167220977709.

4. Michael S. Mooring, Andrew A. McKenzie, and Benjamin L. Hart, "Grooming in Impala: Role of Oral Grooming in Removal of Ticks and Effects of Ticks in Increasing Grooming Rate," *Physiology & Behavior* 59, no. 4–5 (April–May): 965–71, doi.org/10.1016/0031-9384(95)02186-8; Nobuyuki Kutsukake and Tim H. Clutton-Broc, "Social Functions of Allogrooming in Cooperatively Breeding Meerkats," *Animal Behaviour*

72, no. 5 (November 2006): 1059–68, doi.org/10.1016/j.anbehav.2006
.02.016; Markus Port, Dagmar Clough, and Peter M. Kappeler, "Market
Effects Offset the Reciprocation of Grooming in Free-Ranging
Redfronted Lemurs, *Eulemur Fulvus Rufus*," Animal Behaviour 77, no. 1
(January 2009): 29–36, doi.org/10.1016/j.anbehav.2008.08.032.

5. Pawl Fedurek and Robin I. M. Dunbar, "What Does Mutual Grooming
Tell Us About Why Chimpanzees Groom?" *Ethology* 115 (May 2009):
566–575, doi/10.1111/j.1439-0310.2009.01637.

6. Frances A. Champagne et al., "Variations in Maternal Care in the Rat as
a Mediating Influence for the Effects of Environment on Development,"
Physiology and Behavior 79, no. 3. (August 2003): 359–71, doi:10.1016
/s0031-9384(03)00149-510.1016/s0031-9384(03)00149-5; Christian Caldji
et al., "Maternal Care During Infancy Regulates the Development of
Neural Systems Mediating the Expression of Fearfulness in the Rat,"
Proceedings of the National Academy of Sciences 95, no. 9 (April 1998):
5335–40, doi: 10.1073/pnas.95.9.5335.

7. Steven Newcomb, *Pagans in the Promised Land: Decoding the Doctrine
of Christian Discovery* (Chicago: Chicago Review Press//Fulcrum
Publishers, 2008).

8. Ed Fletcher, "California Plans to Replace a Toppled Statue with a
Monument to Native Americans," National Public Radio, October
1, 2021, npr.org/2021/10/01/1042161978/california-plans-to-replace-a
-toppled-statue-with-a-monument-to-native-americans; Kriston Capps,
"Why There Are Still 149 Statues of Christopher Columbus in the U.S.
Bloomberg," Bloomberg.com, October 9, 2021, bloomberg.com/news
/articles/2021-10-09/how-many-statues-of-christopher-columbus-are-left.

9. Dacher Keltner, *Awe: The New Science of Everyday Wonder and How It
Can Transform Your Life* (New York: Penguin Press, 2023).

10. Jack Levison, *A Boundless God: The Spirit According to the Old Testament*
(Ada, MI: Baker Academic, 2020).

11. *Heat, Pneuma, and Soul in Ancient Philosophy and Science*, ed. Hynek Bartoš and Colin Guthrie King (New York: Cambridge University Press, 2020).

12. Aristotle, *De Anima* ed. W. D. Ross (New York: Oxford University Press, 1979).

13. *A History of Mind and Body in Late Antiquity*, ed. Anna Marmodoro and Sophie Cartwright (New York: Cambridge University Press, 2018).

Chapter 10: Heartful Wisdom

1. Gustav Jahoda, "Culture and Psychology: Words and Ideas in History," in *The Oxford Handbook of Culture and Psychology*, ed. Jaan Valsiner (New York: Oxford University Press, 2012).

2. Alan S. Cowen and Dacher Keltner, "Self-Report Captures 27 Distinct Categories of Emotion Bridged by Continuous Gradients," *Proceedings of the National Academy of Sciences* 114, no. 38 (September 2017): E7900–E7909, doi.org/10.1073/pnas.1702247114; Dacher Keltner and Keith Oatley, "Social Functions of Emotions in Life and Imaginative Culture," *Evolutionary Studies in Imaginative Culture* 6, no. 1 (April 2022): 1–20, doi.org/10.26613/esic.6.1.263; Dacher Keltner et al., "How Emotions, Relationships, and Culture Constitute Each Other: Advances in Social Functionalist Theory," *Cognition and Emotion* 36, no. 3 (2022): 388–401, doi.org/10.1080/02699931.2022.2047009.

3. Dacher Keltner, Keith Oatley, and Jennifer M. Jenkins, *Understanding Emotions* (New York: Wiley, 2018).

4. Catriona Sandilands, "Losing My Place: Landscapes of Depression," in *Mourning Nature: Hope at the Heart of Ecological Loss and Grief*, ed. Ashlee Cunsolo and Karen Landman (Montreal: McGill-Queen's University Press, 2017): 144–168; Tim Jensen, "Guilt as Keystone Emotion for Environmental Communication" in *Ecologies of Guilt in Environmental Rhetorics* (London: Palgrave Pivot, 2019): 1–31; Haoran Chu and Janet Z Yang, "Emotion and the Psychological Distance of Climate Change," *Science Communication* 41, no. 6 (December 2019): 761–789, doi.org/10.1177/1075547019889637.

5. Ashlee Cunsolo and Neville R. Ellis, "Ecological Grief as a Mental Health Response to Climate Change–Related Loss," *Nature Climate Change* 8, no. 4 (April 2018): 275–281, doi.org/10.1038/s41558-018 -0092-2; Glenn Albrecht et al., "Solastalgia: The Distress Caused by Environmental Change," *Australasian Psychiatry* 15, no. 1 (February 2007), S95–98, doi.org/10.1080/10398560701701288.

6. Dacher Keltner, *The Power Paradox: How We Gain and Lose Influence* (New York: Penguin, 2016).

7. Damien F. Santomauro et al., "Global Prevalence and Burden of Depressive and Anxiety Disorders in 204 Countries and Territories in 2020 Due to the COVID-19 Pandemic," *The Lancet* 398, no. 10312 (November 2021): 1700–1712, doi.org/10.1016/S0140-6736(21)02143-7.

8. Jean M. Twenge, "Increases in Depression, Self-Harm, and Suicide Among U.S. Adolescents After 2012 and Links to Technology Use: Possible Mechanisms," *Psychiatric Research and Clinical Practice* 2, no. 1 (September 2020): 19–25, doi.org/10.1176/appi.prcp.20190015.

Chapter 11: Ecological Belonging

1. *The Indigenous World 2022*, ed. Dwayne Mamo et al. (International Work Group for Indigenous Affairs, April 2022), iwgia.org/en/documents-and -publications/documents/indigenous-world/english/603-iwgia-book-the -indigenous-world-2022-eng/file.html.

2. Akwesasne Notes, *Basic Call to Consciousness* (Summertown, TN: Native Voices, 2005).

3. Christine Judith Nicholls, "'Dreamtime' and 'The Dreaming'—An Introduction," The Conversation.com, January 22, 2014, theconversation .com/dreamtime-and-the-dreaming-an-introduction-20833.

4. Qing Li, "Effect of Forest Bathing Trips on Human Immune Function," *Environmental Health and Preventive Medicine* 15, no. 1 (January 2010): 9–17, ncbi.nlm.nih.gov/pmc/articles/PMC2793341.

5. Margaret M. Hansen, Reo Jones, and Kirsten Tocchi, "Shinrin-Yoku (Forest Bathing) and Nature Therapy: A State-of-the-Art Review," *Environmental Research and Public Health* 14, no. 8 (August 2017): 851, doi.org.10.3390/ijerph14080851; E. Morita et al., "Psychological Effects of Forest Environments on Healthy Adults: Shinrin-yoku (Forest-Air Bathing, Walking) as a Possible Method of Stress Reduction," *Public Health* 121, no. 1 (January 2007): 54–63, doi: 10.1016/j.puhe.2006.05.024; Hiroko Ochiai et al., "Physiological and Psychological Effects of Forest Therapy on Middle-Aged Males with High-Normal Blood Pressure," *Environmental Research and Public Health* 12, no. 3 (February 2015): 2532–3542, doi: 10.3390/ijerph120302532.

6. Chia-Pin Yu et al., "Effects of Short Forest Bathing Program on Autonomic Nervous System Activity and Mood States in Middle-Aged and Elderly Individuals," *International Journal of Environmental Research and Public Health* 14, no. 8 (August 2017): 897, ncbi.nlm.nih .gov/pmc/articles/PMC5579495/; J. Lee et al., "Effect of Forest Bathing on Physiological and Psychological Responses in Young Japanese Male Subjects," *Public Health* 125, no. 2 (February 2011): 93–100, ncbi.nlm.nih .gov/pmc/articles/PMC2793341.

7. Luciana Porter-Bolland et al., "Community-Managed Forests and Forest-Protected Areas: An Assessment of Their Conservation Effectiveness Across the Tropics," *Forest Ecology and Management* 268 (March 2012): 6–17, doi.org/10.1016/j.foreco.2011.05.034.

8. *Forest Governance by Indigenous and Tribal People: An Opportunity for Climate Action in Latin America and the Caribbean* (Santiago, Chile: Food and Agriculture Organzation of the United Nations, 2021), doi.org /10.4060/cb2953en.

9. *Forest Governance by Indigenous and Tribal People: An Opportunity for Climate Action in Latin America and the Caribbean* (Santiago, Chile: Food and Agriculture Organization of the United Nations, 2021).

10. *II Congreso Nacional de Tierras Comunales*, Grupo Promotor de Tierras Comunales, 2020, cdc.usac.edu.gt/wp-content/uploads/2020/12/GPTC -II-Congreso-Nacional-de-Tierras-Comunales.pdf.

11. "Joint Tripartite (FAO, OIE, WHO) and UNEP Statement Tripartite and UNEP support OHHLEP's definition of 'One Health,'" United Nations Food and Agriculture Organization of the United Nations (FAO), the World Organisation for Animal Health (OIE), the United Nations Environment Programme (UNEP), and the World Health Organization (WHO), 2017, wedocs.unep.org/bitstream/handle/20.500.11822/37600/JTFOWU.pdf.

12. "Declaration of Astana," Global Conference on Primary Health Care, United Nations World Health Organization and United Nations Children's Fund, 2018, who.int/docs/default-source/primary-health/declaration/gcphc-declaration.pdf.

13. Angola Andorra et al., "The Human Right to a Clean, Healthy, and Sustainable Environment," United Nations, July 26, 2022, digitallibrary.un.org/record/3982508; "United Nations Environment Assembly Agrees Nature-Based Solutions Definition," Nature-Based Solutions Initiative.org, March 3, 2022, naturebasedsolutionsinitiative.org/news/united-nations-environment-assembly-nature-based-solutions-definition.

14. *High and Rising Mortality Rates Among Working-Age Adults*, National Academies of Sciences, Engineering, and Medicine (Washington, DC: The National Academies Press, 2021), doi.org/10.17226/25976.

15. *The Sustainable Development Goals Report 2022* (New York: United Nations Publications, 2022), unstats.un.org/sdgs/report/2022/The-Sustainable-Development-Goals-Report-2022.pdf.

16. "Front Line Defenders," Front Line Defenders.org., frontlinedefenders.org.

17. *The Indigenous World 2022*, ed. Dwayne Mamo, International Work Group for Indigenous Affairs, iwgia.org/en/documents-and-publications/documents/indigenous-world/english/603-iwgia-book-the-indigenous-world-2022-eng/file.html.

18. Ana Esther Ceceña and David Barrios, "Mexico's War on Drugs as a Policy of Social Reorganization," May 6, 2022, International Work

Group for Indigenous Affairs News, iwgia.org/en/news/4778-mexico
-s-war-on-drugs-as-a-policy-of-social-reorganization.html; Gilberto
López Y Rivas, "Indigenous Peoples of Latin America in the Light
of Drug Trafficking," April 26, 2022, International Work Group for
Indigenous Affairs News, iwgia.org/en/news/4724-indigenous-peoples
-of-latin-america-in-the-light-of-drug-trafficking.html; "Report of the
Special Rapporteur on the Rights of Indigenous Peoples on Her Visit to
Mexico—Note by the Secretariat," UN Human Rights Council Special
Rapporteur on Rights of Indigenous Peoples and UN Human Rights
Council, June 28, 2018, documents-dds-ny.un.org/doc/UNDOC/GEN
/G18/192/94/PDF/G1819294.pdf?OpenElement.

19. "Non-Discrimination: Groups in Vulnerable Situations: Special
Rapporteur on the Right to Health," United Nations Office of the High
Commissioner on Human Rights, OCHR.org, ohchr.org/en/special
-procedures/sr-health/non-discrimination-groups-vulnerable-situations.

20. "The 3rd Declaration for Health, Lie, and Defense of Our Lands, Rights,
and Future Generations," International Indigenous Women's Symposium
on Environmental and Reproductive Health: Advancing Research and
Assessing Impacts of Environmental Violence on Indigenous Women
and Girls, April 2018, humanrightscolumbia.org/sites/default/files/pdf
/indigenous_symposium_declaration_2018_eng.pdf.

21. Jonathan Loh and David Harmon, *Biocultural Diversity: Threatened
Species, Endangered Languages* (Zeist, The Netherlands: World Wildlife
Fund, 2014), wwfint.awsassets.panda.org/downloads/biocultural
_report__june_2014.pdf; Brendan Mackey and David Claudie, "Points
of Contact: Integrating Traditional and Scientific Knowledge for
Biocultural Conservation," *Environmental Ethics* 37, no. 3 (2015): 341–357,
doi.org/10.5840/enviroethics201537332; Krystyna Swiderska, Alejandro
Argumedo, and Michel Pimbert, "Biocultural Heritage Territories: Key
to Halting Biodiversity Loss," International Institute for Environment
and Development Briefing, July 2020, iied.org/17760iied.

22. "10 Things to Know about Indigenous Peoples," United Nations Development Program, July 29, 2021, stories.undp.org/10-things-we-all -should-know-about-indigenous-people.

23. The United Nations is conformed of 192 member states and two non-member states (The Holy See and the State of Palestine). The United States and the Holy See did not attend the UN Global Biodiversity Conference and did not sign the Global Biodiversity Framework of December of 2022.

Chapter 12: Reparations Through Right Relationships

1. Gail B, Mahady, "Global Harmonization of Herbal Health Claims," *Journal of Nutrition* 131, no. 3 (March 2001): 1120S–1123S, doi.org/10.1093 /jn/131.3.1120S.

2. "Medicinal Botany," US Forest Service, fs.usda.gov/wildflowers /ethnobotany/medicinal/index.shtml; *Modern Phytomedicine: Turning Medicinal Plants into Drugs*, ed. Iqbal Ahmad, Farrukh Aqil, and Mohammad Owais (New York: Wiley, 2006), doi.org/10.1002 /9783527609987.

3. Yuria Celidwen et al., "Ethical Principles of Traditional Indigenous Medicine to Guide Western Psychedelic Research and Practice," *The Lancet Regional Health: Americas* 18 (February 2023), doi.org/10.1016/j .lana.2022.100410.

4. Modified from Yuria Celidwen et al., "Ethical Principles of Traditional Indigenous Medicine to Guide Western Psychedelic Research and Practice."

5. Expanded from the eight ethical principles originally presented in Yuria Celidwen et al., "Ethical Principles of Traditional Indigenous Medicine to Guide Western Psychedelic Research and Practice."

Recommended Resources
by Yuria Celidwen

Selected Publications

Yuria Celidwen et al., "Ethical Principles of Traditional Indigenous Medicine to Guide Western Psychedelic Research and Practice," *The Lancet Regional Health: Americas* 18 (December 16, 2022); doi.org/10.1016/j.lana.2022.100410.

Yuria Celidwen, "Radical Ecstasy: The Passionate Compassion of Sacred Altruism," PhD diss., Pacifica Graduate Institute, 2020.

Yuria Celidwen and Dacher Keltner, "Kin Relationality and Ecological Belonging: A Cultural Psychology of Indigenous Transcendence," *Frontiers in Psychology* 14 (October 2023); doi.org/10.3389/fpsyg.2023.994508.

Yuria Celidwen, "Mictlan, Our Shared Home: Funerary Rites and the Contemplative Experience in Indigenous Mexico," in *The Routledge International Handbook of Research Methods in Spirituality & Contemplative Studies* (New York: Routledge, 2024).

Yuria Celidwen, "Why We Need Indigenous Wisdom," mindandlife.org, Mind & Life Institute, September 7, 2022; mindandlife.org/insight/why-we-need-indigenous-wisdom.

Yuria Celidwen, "Semillas del Resurgimiento: Sabiduría Indígena Contemplativa y Bienestar Colectivo Sostenible," in *El Desarrollo Humano y La Protección de Los Derechos Humanos en Poblaciones Vulnerables* (Madrid: Dykinson, 2022).

Yuria Celidwen, "Women Weaver-of-Worlds: Earth-Based Mythopoesis in Restorative Indigenous Narratives," in *Valuing Lives, Healing Earth: Religion, Gender, and Life on Earth*, edited by Theresa A. Yugar et al., (Leuven, Belgium: Peeters Publishers, 2021).

Yuria Celidwen, "Special Issue on Chinese-Latinx / Latinx-Chinese," *Chinese America, History & Perspectives*, 2021: 5–11.

Yuria Celidwen, "Tonantzin Coatlicue Guadalupe: Symbolism, Colonization, and Social Justice," in *Vibrant Voices: Women, Myth, and the Arts* (Proceedings of the Association for the Study of Women and Mythology, 2018); womenandmyth.org/2018/03/11/vibrant-voices-anthology-released.

Ivan Natividad, "Why Indigenous Spirit Medicine Principles Must be a Priority in Psychedelic Research," on the work of Yuria Celidwen, Berkeley News; news.berkeley.edu/2023/05/03/why-indigenous-spirit-medicine-principles-must-be-a-priority-in-psychedelic-research.

Nicole Redvers, Paula Aubrey, Yuria Celidwen, and Kyle Hill, "Indigenous Peoples: Traditional Knowledges, Climate Change, and Health," edited by Madhukar Pai, *PLOS Global Public Health* 3 (October 13, 2023); doi.org/10.1371/journal.pgph.0002474.

Nicole Redvers, Yuria Celidwen, Quanah Yellow Cloud et al., "Indigenous Solutions to the Climate and Biodiversity Crises: A Reflection on UNDRIP," edited by Julia Robinson, *PLOS Global Public Health* 3 (June 14, 2023); doi.org/10.1371/journal.pgph.0002060.

Nicole Redvers, Yuria Celidwen, Clinton Schultz et al., "The Determinants of Planetary Health: An Indigenous Consensus Perspective," *The Lancet Planetary Health* 6, no. 2 (February 2022); doi.org/10.1016/S2542-5196 (21)00354-5.

State of the World's Indigenous Peoples, Volume V, Rights to Lands, Territories and Resources (New York: United Nations, DESA, 2021).

State of the World's Indigenous Peoples, Volume IV, Implementing the United Nations Declaration on the Rights of Indigenous Peoples (New York: United Nations, DESA, 2019).

State of the World's Indigenous Peoples, Volume III, Education United Nations (New York: United Nations, DESA, 2017).

State of the World's Indigenous Peoples, Volume II, Health United Nations (New York: United Nations, DESA, 2016).

State of the World's Indigenous Peoples, Volume I United Nations (New York: United Nations, DESA, 2009).

Selected Videos

Yuria Celidwen, "Ethics of Belonging of Indigenous Contemplative Traditions," Mindfulness and Anti-Racism Lecture Series, Kathryn M. Buder Center for American Indian Studies, 2024, Brown School at Washington University, YouTube video, youtube.com/watch?v=VC29hS9cljQ.

Yuria Celidwen, "The Ethics of Belonging of Indigenous Traditions," Bioneers Conference, Berkeley, California, April 8, 2023, YouTube video, youtube.com/watch?v=yOniXorjCho.

Yuria Celidwen, "Reconnection to Self, Soul, and Earth: An Indigenous Contemplative Practice," February 16, 2021, YouTube video, youtube.com/watch?v=521ZdV8UxBI.

Naomi Klein, Bayo Akomolaf, and Yuria Celidwen, "Climate Grief and Hope," UC Berkeley Othering and Belonging Institute, May, 2023, YouTube video, youtube.com/watch?v=sW4-i7Givao.

Yuria Celidwen, "The Ethics of Belonging: An Indigenous Perspective," Wisdom 2.0 Conference, April 2023, YouTube video, youtube.com/watch?v=kiPcAaCMMYA&t=1s.

OHRP Exploratory Workshop 2023: "Exploring the Ethical and Practical Considerations of Psychedelics Research," September 14, 2023, Videocast, videocast.nih.gov/watch=49708&start=16278.

"Religious and Spiritual Engagement: Building Connected Communities," Foundation for Social Connection, October 16, 2023, YouTube video, youtube.com/watch?v=6eTPjidE3Eo.

"Science and Wisdom of Emotions Summit with His Holiness the Dalai Lama," The Awake Network and Mind & Life Institute, May 2021, scienceandwisdomofemotions.com.

Yuria Celidwen, "Indigenous Contemplative Science: An Ethics of Belonging and Reconnection," The Center for Contemplative Mind in Society, May 29, 2020, YouTube video, youtube.com/watch?v=nJNNKLeB57g.

"Conversation With Yuria Celidwen, Nahuat, and Mayan Chiapas," Two Legged Experience, February 7, 2022, YouTube video, youtube.com/watch?v=Qv-yAGrJmA8.

Selected Podcasts

Yuria Celidwen with Dahr Jamail, "Dismantling Destructive Narratives," December 5, 2023, *Holding the Fire: Indigenous Voices on the Great Unraveling*, holdingthefire.buzzsprout.com/2248159/14073387.

Yuria Celidwen, "Visions of Hope: Intergenerational Wisdom for a Flourishing Planet," September 2023, *Into the Magic Shop*, with Dr. James Doty, available at open.spotify.com/episode/oL2u6ycCsy6LQdabaoN73x?si=gdakTelRR_is-h3g7fetpQ.

Yuria Celidwen, "Indigenous Wisdom," October 21, 2022, *Mind & Life Podcast*, available at podcast.mindandlife.org/yuria-celidwen.

"Happiness Break: A Meditation to Connect to Your Roots, with Yuria Celidwen," August 25, 2022, *The Science of Happiness*, available at open.spotify.com/episode/oskN95RShk1CAQXfnFZeDn

"Happiness Break: How to Ground Yourself, with Yuria Celidwen," May 5, 2022, *The Science of Happiness*, available at open.spotify.com/episode/5QDlgtBrFd7NEgOZpbkO2t.

Yuria Celidwen, "How to Advance the Rights of the Earth and Indigenous People," May 2022, *The Nuance* by Medicine Explained, available at podcasts.apple.com/us/podcast/68-how-to-advance-the-rights-of-the-earth/id1537453361?i=1000568910486.

Yuria Celidwen, "Self-Transcendence," March 2022, *The Contemplative Science Podcast*, Episode 3, thecontemplativescientists.com/episodes /episode-02-peakcbd-xcfkb.

"How Awe Cultivates Community in Indigenous Cultures," August 7, 2021, Jonathan Bastian interviews Yuria Celidwen, *Life Examined*, kcrw.com /culture/shows/life-examined/awe-happiness-purpose-indigenous -peoples/yuria-celinwen-indigenous-cultures-social-behavior.

Yuria Celidwen, "Prácticas Contemplativas Indígenas," May 2021, Episode 19, *Biodegradable*, available at open.spotify.com/episode /3CMN3Rvy2XGoVVIgu4u9nt?si=huWtVbaLSsmKLR3HWvBmqw& dl_branch=1&nd=1.

"Are You Listening to Your Elders?" December 10, 2020, Episode 81, *The Science of Happiness*, available at greatergood.berkeley.edu/podcasts/item /are_you_listening_to_your_elders_cafe_ohlone.

"Happiness Break: How to Be in Harmony in Nature—Wherever You Are." with Yuria Celidwen, May, 2023. *The Science of Happiness*, available at greatergood.berkeley.edu/podcasts/item/belonging_to_the_earth_with _yuria_celidwen.

"How to Do Good for the Environment (And Yourself)," May 2023, *The Science of Happiness*, available at open.spotify.com/episode /5DFpxfixOjWhWy3Ajd9BE6?si=pVkqMjPDS9OBbiO6dEvOng.

About the Author

I AM A NATIVE of Indigenous Nahua and Maya lineages, born into a family of mystics, healers, poets, and explorers of sacred Land, body, and soul from the highlands of Chiapas, Mexico. I grew up with one foot in the wilderness and another in magical realism. My Elders' songs and stories enthralled my childhood. They enhanced my mythic imagination, inquisitive curiosity, and emotional intuition, which became the fertile soil where the seeds of kindness, play, wonder, and scholarship dug their roots.

My scholarship focuses on the intersection of Indigenous studies, religious studies, cultural psychology, contemplative science, human rights, and decolonial studies, thus being naturally transdisciplinary in scope and aims. Through qualitative research using Indigenous epistemologies and methodologies, I approach the experience of self-transcendence by examining how it varies across Indigenous traditions in its embodiment and enhancement of prosocial and other-focused behavior (ethics, compassion, reverence, and a sense of awe, sacredness, and love). From the substantial attention to the components of participatory research, I uncover Indigenous forms of contemplation from around the world and reclaim their place as practices of self and social transformation.

My career of almost two decades at the United Nations supports international humanitarian efforts to implement the Sustainable Development Goals and advance Indigenous Peoples' rights and the rights of Nature. From this work, I have cultivated a robust network of collaborators with faith leaders and activists from Indigenous traditions worldwide. The materials we create are distributed globally and reach vast audiences, from heads of state to academic institutions and the general public. In addition, I established the first long-term contemplative workshops (mindfulness and compassion training) for UN staff, reaching all duty stations worldwide.

From my work on Indigenous contemplative science, I developed insights into Indigenous religious traditions of the world, acquiring an innovative understanding of religion that challenges the Western paradigm. This framework pays attention to contextual and cultural aspects of the experience of the sacred through the lens of Indigenous traditions. My work investigates community knowledge and practice-based journeys to cultivate a sense of sacredness in everyday life. My approach is contemplative. A respectful introduction to Indigenous science, methodologies, and spirituality leads the audience to reflect on ethical values, the complex associations between colonization and religion, reverence and Land awareness, and social and environmental responsibility as paths to a collective, participatory, and meaningful spiritual life.

I work through epistemological equity methods that bridge Indigenous and Western sciences to complement each other based on qualitative and quantitative research, generating capacities for a meaningful pursuit of and reflection on the religious and spiritual life. I teach Indigenous forms of contemplation, epistemologies, and spirituality in academic settings and for lay audiences. My pioneering work on Indigenous contemplative experiences brings to light prosocial and planetary flourishing practices from an Indigenous perspective. With this, I mean learning how to be responsibly humane as a process of discovery, which takes a commitment to analyzing the stories that have been imposed upon us. Then, we engage in a caring journey of reckoning, reparation, and compassionate stewarding of the world, communities, and our own selves.

The contemplative method I invite us to consider involves critical thinking and careful reasoning into how our identities have been conditioned by our cultures and how we project our cultural values onto our perception of ourselves and the world. I approach my research and pedagogies from a transdisciplinary perspective, which brings together the fullness of the human experience from those fields that most impact identity-formation. I believe that achieving learning and well-being by establishing an ethical code of conduct of communal support is essential in our interaction with our shared home planet. This collaborative stance reflects a quest for reflection from multiple dimensions specific to our time and space. As cultures cross-pollinate, we adapt and transform. Therefore, it becomes crucial to examine how religious practices are impacted by the intersection of cultures, genders, and political movements to understand the dynamism and dialectical richness of humanity's sociocultural expressions.

My pedagogic style is unusual because it introduces Indigenous methodologies and epistemologies into the learning environment. This intentional stance is my commitment to give voice to those ways of being that have been left silent due to systems of erasure and oppression that overlook in the same way neurodivergent needs and learning styles of all audiences. My aim is to design materials that offer an opportunity for an experiential and engaged form of learning as a living and dynamic process that considers continuous struggles of discrimination based on racial, ethnic, gender, sexuality, class, special needs, and religious diversity. I am strongly motivated to bring awareness of the imperatives of tolerance, equity, and respect in a growingly pluralistic and diverse world.

About Sounds True

SOUNDS TRUE WAS founded in 1985 by Tami Simon with a clear mission: to disseminate spiritual wisdom. Since starting out as a project with one woman and her tape recorder, we have grown into a multimedia publishing company with a catalog of more than 3,000 titles by some of the leading teachers and visionaries of our time, and an ever-expanding family of beloved customers from across the world.

In more than three decades of evolution, Sounds True has maintained our focus on our overriding purpose and mission: to wake up the world. We offer books, audio programs, online learning experiences, and in-person events to support your personal growth and awakening, and to unlock our greatest human capacities to love and serve.

At SoundsTrue.com you'll find a wealth of resources to enrich your journey, including our weekly *Insights at the Edge* podcast, free downloads, and information about our nonprofit Sounds True Foundation, where we strive to remove financial barriers to the materials we publish through scholarships and donations worldwide.

To learn more, please visit SoundsTrue.com/freegifts or call us toll-free at 800.333.9185.

Together, we can wake up the world.

About Sounds True